Fond Hopes Destroyed

Fond Hopes Destroyed

Breach of Promise Cases in Shetland
1823 - 1900

Mary Prior

The Shetland Times Ltd.
Lerwick
2005

Fond Hopes Destroyed – Breach of Promise Cases in Shetland

ISBN 1 904746 09 8

First published by The Shetland Times Ltd., 2005.

British Library Cataloguing-in-Publication Data
A catalogue record for this book is available from the British Library.

Cover photographs:
Front – Woman on doorstep c.1890's. © Shetland Museum (A00272)
Back – Waiting for the steamer, Hillswick, 1900. © Shetland Museum (00086WB)

Published and printed by
The Shetland Times Ltd.,
Gremista, Lerwick,
Shetland ZE1 0PX.

Contents

Illustrations

Letters reproduced by kind permission of Shetland Archives.

Introduction

I first visited Shetland twenty-five years ago, seizing the opportunity to visit this most northern part of Britain presented by my daughter working at the Fair Isle Bird Observatory. It was a cold wet summer and I did not take to it. However, my daughter settled in Shetland, and it is now over ten years since I bought a cottage in Scalloway where I spend my summers. The changes which have taken place in Shetland have been enormous. Although North Sea oil had brought incomers and greater prosperity from the seventies, the transformation it would bring was slow to be reflected even in the eighties. Those in the oil industry lived mainly in the north of the Mainland, and most Shetlanders did not. Traditional life continued, perhaps even intensified in the face of competition. Shetlanders might emigrate, but as they became more prosperous bus loads of them crossed the world to visit their cousins abroad, and those living abroad came over individually or in number to Hamefarins which kept their links with Shetland strong. It was a different world to that in which Shetland men and women lived in the nineteenth and early twentieth centuries.

Then long and dangerous voyages by sea divided sailors from their families and sweethearts. And the letters they sent home to their sweethearts are full of enquiries about friends and family at home, and give news of Shetlanders met abroad. They suggest a high level of homesickness, which is to some extent an artifact. We learn nothing of life on shipboard; no doubt familiarity bred boredom, while, if a sailor had a girl in every port, this was not to be mentioned. Their letters to their sweethearts might provide evidence which could form the basis for a case of Breach of Promise. Those who stayed at home seldom wrote letters, though one wrote from Whalsay to Lerwick, and one from one side of a voe to the other. Where there were no letters expenditure on food or drink for the wedding breakfast or on a wedding dress might provide evidence.

When I started work on this subject three or four summers ago I decided to hide the identity of the people involved in these cases, and I did so by only giving the initials of their surnames, so hoping to spare the feelings of their kin. I now think this was a bit quixotic. Shetlanders are tougher than that, and anyway it is not difficult to work out who they

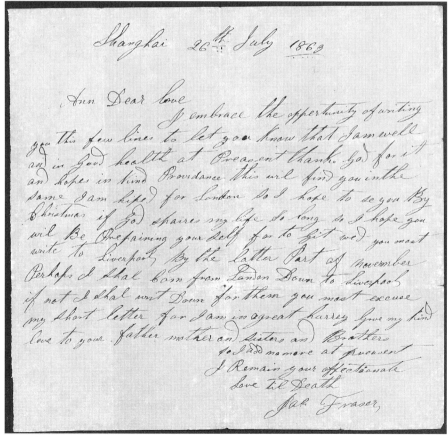

A joyfully incriminating letter.

were; they were real people, and their feelings were ones we might have had in their place. I abandoned the scheme.

The law permitting Breach of Promise cases in Scotland was rescinded in 1984. It is odd to think that cases could still be brought when I first visited Shetland, but the action was very rare in the twentieth century.

I should like to thank many people who have provided help and friendship over the years. Brian Smith and Angus Johnson of the Shetland Archives have taught me so much of what I know of Shetland, and Joan Thirsk who had supervised my thesis and visited Shetland many times has always been a tower of strength. Margaret Robertson has shared with me her knowledge of Shetland's sons and daughters. John Graham and George Peterson have provided information on particular families, and Wendy Gear introduced me to the Bride of Vigon. And not least the women of the Youth Hostel's café, which provided the setting for many discussions over morning tea. My daughter has patiently word-processed my fumbling typescript. Finally my thanks to Charlotte Black for helpful editorial suggestions and help over the illustrations.

Chapter 1

Fond Hopes Destroyed

The marriage day was fixed, the wedding dresses were bought, the wedding tour was planned out, the wedding guests were invited, the day came, but not the groom.[1]

Dickens sketched with masterly economy the situation out of which a case of breach of promise might arise. According to both Scottish civil and ecclesiastical law whatever promises might have been made, either party might renegue up to the last moment. No one could be forced into a union unwillingly.[2] This is well illustrated by a Shetland case noted in the North Yell parish register. Charles Rusland was to marry Barbara Brown on the forenoon of the 24th May, 1823.[3] The banns had been proclaimed, and pawns paid.[4] Friends assembled at Vigon for the contract feast on the Saturday before the wedding.[5] However, James Sinclair, a former sweetheart, sent a lad in to the feast to persuade Barbara to come outside to talk to him. She left the guests, slipped out of the house and went with him to the Precentor's house. Here they lodged a line for their pawns, and paid a fee for calling the

---

1   Charles Dickens, *Great Expectations*, chapter 22. For a full blown case see Pickwick's own case in *Pickwick Papers*, passim. Such cases occur in many Victorian novels, and mentions of them are frequent. The Victorians were fascinated by the subject.

2   R. Mitchison and L. Leneman, *Sexuality and Control: Scotland 1660-1780* (Basil Blackwell, 1989), pp. 82-3.

3   Shetland Archives, North Yell Parish register, 1754-1854, microfilm of Scottish Record office, OPR 4/5. Cf. *The Orcadian*, 25 Aug. 1868.

4   Pawns or consignation money was deposited as a guarantee of good behaviour.

5   P. Fraser, 'Old-Time Shetland Day Wedding' (*Shetland Folk Book*, vol. 3, 1957), p. 58.

banns, which were called the next day at the kirk at Cullivoe. Charles Rusland 'contrary to the advice of his friends made no objection.' The following day the minister heard the case, and caused the banns to be read again three times. And so, on Sunday 25th May James Sinclair and Barbara Brown were married.

Charles Rusland did not object, despite the advice of his friends. For he had no grounds. The girl could not be forced to marry him. He could, however, have brought a breach of promise case against her in the Sheriff court, which came to have jurisdiction over these cases from that very year.[6] But he did not. Indeed no man brought a case of breach of promise against a woman in Shetland in the Sheriff Court as far as we know and it was rare in England. In her study of English cases in the late nineteenth century, which seems to have been based on a very large sample, Ginger Frost found they made up only 3% of the total.[7] There were in all 25 cases in Shetland between 1823 and 1900, all but one brought by women, and that brought by the father of a dead girl.[8] As the defender simply went away to sea it never came to court. For a man to bring a case involved him at the very least in public ridicule. For such cases aired in court attracted a ribald audience, destroying a man's self-respect. The fear of being sued however must have forced many men into loveless marriages, whatever their social standing. The case of Edward Irving provides an example. He was the charismatic minister of a kirk in Regent Square to whose sermons fashionable London flocked in the late 1820's and early 1830's. He married Isabella Martin daughter of the minister of Kirkcaldy in 1823 after an eleven-year engagement. But in 1821 he had fallen deeply in love with Jane Walsh, the brilliant

6   In 1823 jurisdiction over breach of promise cases passed from the Commissary Courts to the Sheriff Courts. The first Shetland case was commenced on the 5th of March 1823: Shetland Archives, SC 12/6/1823/13.

7   G.S. Frost, 'I shall not sit down and crie': Women, class and Breach of Promise of Marriage plaintiffe in England, 1850-1900', (*Gender and History* vol. 6, no. 2, 1994), p. 225. This is a very rich and instructive paper, but the English situation was often very different. This paper does not attempt to make comparisons.

8   Shetland Archives, SC 12/6/1891/15.

young woman who later married Thomas Carlyle. He asked the Martin family to release him from his engagement, which they refused, and he made the best of things and married Miss Martin.[9]

The Shetland Context of Breach of Promise Cases

For a woman the position was very different. Marriage was seen as the highest goal for a woman, and this was especially true in Shetland. Apart from a small group of professional and commercial families, the bulk of the population farmed, and the men of the family were fishermen and seamen, some being absent seasonally, others far across the sea for years at a time. The working of the farm was left to the family, and the wife assumed direction of its affairs. To them fell an endless round of toil: crops must be grown to feed the family, the animals must be cared for and their wool spun and knitted up to sell or barter to supply the goods the farm could not supply. The mortality of the men was high, for seafaring was, and is, a high risk occupation. Early last century Christina Jamieson noted the psychological effects of this situation on women:

The interest and variety of their lives are supplied by the men. Their daughters, like the poor, are always with them, and only follow their lead in the monotonous and unprogressive rounds of indoor and outdoor toil... But the sons who come and go – it is they who make the hearts beat and the eyes light up.

And again:

The whole interest, effort, ambition and tragedy of their lives centre on the men, whose lives are so precarious.[10]

The marriage prospects of women were unusually bleak, for there was a considerable surplus of women in the population. In the Far North

9   *Dictionary of National Biography* – Edward Irving,
10   C. Jamieson, 'The women of Shetland, (*The Shetland News*, 22 and 29 Jan. 1910, reprinted in *The New Shetlander*, no. 177, 1991).

(Orkney and Shetland taken together), the proportion of men to women was lower than anywhere else in Scotland, and at its lowest in 1861 and 1871.[11] In those years there were only 82 men to every 100 women of all ages. In the period when women were most fertile, from 15-49, the proportion in 1861 was 71 men to 100 women, and 72 in 1871. By 1901 it had risen to between 80 and 90 in each of the three selected age groups.[12] Some interesting deductions could be made from these figures if they are combined with the statistics on the percentage of selected male groups and of female groups married from 1861 onwards. For much of the period between 1861 and 1931 few more than two out of three women in the Far North married during their reproductive period. With men it was far otherwise. With such a wide choice of possible spouses a high proportion of men might be expected to marry, but the proportion marrying was close to the national average. There was in fact a reluctance to marry on the part of men.[13]

Flinn puts this reluctance of the men to marry in part to economic factors; but it was not just a matter of low pay. Despite the fact that in a seafaring community where men's lives were seen as precarious, and there was much migration as well, men were the centre of women's adulation, and interest.[14] Life at home might appear attractive, yet another factor may have been at work which explains this reluctance to marry. The men may have felt smothered by love.

For young women the only work available was hard and not very remunerative. If she was one of a small family, or an only daughter, working unpaid within the house or on the family's land would be almost inevitable. Other daughters might work as servants, perhaps as shop-girls, or, after mid-century, when the herring trade was flourishing,

---

11 The following statistics are taken from M. Flinn et al., *Scottish Population History 1500 to 1630* (Cambridge, 1977), and are based on the Census.
12 Flinn, pp. 318-9.
13 Flinn, pp. 324-7.
14 See Jamieson, op. cit.

as gippers.[15] For them marriage did not provide an easier life, but it gave them a higher standing in the community, as mothers and matriarchs, and the power within the family of decision making in the absence of their husbands, and very often in their presence. It was they who usually held the purse strings.[16]

An analysis of the occupations of the women who brought these cases underlines how limited were their opportunities, and in this they probably did not differ markedly from other Shetland women; eight of the 25 were servants; one, a 'tenant', must have presumably had a landholding of her own; another was a gipper, and the occupations of the rest were not given. It is most likely they were living and working in their families' houses and on their land. The servants were a mixed bunch. Three probably regarded themselves as superior servants. They worked for lairds, one having a sister who married one of them. All three gave up their positions in expectation of marrying, as did others. The gipper was one of three women who had a connection with the herring trade in the 1880's; the other two were jilted by coopers.

The main occupation of the men was connected with the sea. Fifteen men called themselves sailors, seamen or fishermen. The three whose occupations are unknown may have been tenant farmers or crofters. There was also a dyke-builder, a country shopkeeper, and a Lerwick gardener. The variety of jobs available for men was wider than for women.

As no comparable study of breach of promise for any other area of Scotland has been done so far as I am aware, it is not possible to estimate whether the number of cases in Shetland was abnormally high or not, but it would seem that seafarers were particularly vulnerable to

---

15   S. Telford '*In a World a wir ane': A Shetland Herring Girl's Story* (The Shetland Times Ltd, 1998), pp. 1-6; M. Bochel, '*Dear Gremista': the Story of the Nairn Fisher Girls at the Gutting* (National Museum of Antiquities of Scotland, for Nairn Fishertown Museum, 1979). The demands on the servant were perhaps not as unrealistic as is suggested by 'The duties of the chambermaid', Shetland Archives, D 8/400/16, archive of Bruce of Sumburgh. Bruce was a laird; but the life of a farm servant would be as demanding as that of her sister in the lairds' house.

16   See Jamieson, op. cit.

charges of breach of promise because the letters of home-sick men far from home provided jilted girls with ammunition.

If there were no letters, winning a case was more difficult. As the agent of one jilted girl pointed out, 'a direct promise of marriage in the early stages of courtship, although clearly understood, is a matter naturally kept secret between the parties themselves'.[17] However, according to Bell's Dictionary, it could be inferred from a course of conduct.[18] That others accepted the fact that that they were engaged, if neither party denied it, was another ground. The buying of clothes for the wedding, or of food for the feast, were others, whilst of course, the bidding of the banns (as in the case of the bride of Vigon), was a public declaration of intention.[19] Letters or no letters, only two Shetland women lost their cases in the Sheriff Court.[20]

It was in the period of courting, when a girl's expectation's were raised high, that things might go wrong, and promises of marriage and of love 'till death' be broken. This was particularly cruel for Shetland girls for if the hope of marriage was disappointed once, the opportunity was unlikely to recur, while for the men there was still a wide choice. And traditionally it was he who proposed. She could not seek out a new match. There was a cruel asymmetry in the situation.

And yet young men and women mixed on terms of easy familiarity and apparent equality. Courtships, carried out in the winter months, when the fishing season had ended, were, perforce, indoor affairs. The men joined the girls at night and they gossiped together for hours in bed. The cold made bed a comfortable place to talk, and clothes were not removed, it was said. Shetland houses usually consisted of no more than two rooms, and the bed was often shared with a sister, or the room

---

17   SC 12/6/1823/13/9, p.2.
18   *Bell's Dictionary and Digest of the Law of Scotland,* (Bell and Barfute, Edinburgh, 1882, New Edn., ed G. Wilson), p.627.
19   Ibid.
20   SC 12/6/1823/13/9, p. 2; SC 12/6/1894/24/4

shared with others.[21] The immorality of these 'country courtships' was strongly condemned by the middle class.[22] However the illegitimacy rate in Shetland was lower than anywhere else in Scotland, save Ross, which had a comparable rate, so these strictures were clearly unjustified.[23]

The Courts and Breach of Promise Cases

Originally these cases were handled by church courts. The parish kirks dealt with the sins of most parishioners from Sabbath breaking to sex, and breach of promise fell within their remit. Humble women accused of fornication would frequently claim they had been seduced 'under promise of marriage', naming the individual. The Session would try to persuade the man to marry the girl, and if he would not, to support the child. Church discipline would be imposed on both, but less heavily on the girl. The man who evaded his responsibilities would probably be excommunicated. Though the Kirk is often seen as sex-obsessed by its critics, yet it attempted to see that women who were taken advantage of were granted some protection. Penitents, whether male or female, were received back into the fold once penance was done to the satisfaction of the Session.[24] In Lerwick the Kirk Session Minute Books show that women and their guilty partners were haled before the Kirk Session almost to the end of the nineteenth century.[25] Seventeen women claimed to have been seduced under promise of marriage, and sought aliment from their erstwhile lovers. The best the Kirk could do for the women was to reconcile them with their seducers, and three successful cases are

21   *Shetland News*, 10 Mar. 1894; 26 May 1894; 13 April 1889.
22   *The Shetland Times*, 23 and 30 March 1889.
23   T.C. Smout, 'Aspects of Sexual Behaviour in 19th century Scotland', in A. A. Maclaren, ed., *Social Class in Scotland* (John Donald, Edinburgh, 1974), pp. 75-6; Flinn, pp. 350-1.
24   Mitchison and Leneman, *Sexuality and Social Control: Scotland 1660-1780*, pp. 88-93. For an 1753 case in Lerwick brought by a man see Shetland Archives, CH 2/1072/1, pp. 83-0. I am grateful to Emma Mulley for this reference.
25   Shetland Archives, CH 2/1072/3, 1780-1842; CH 2/1072/13, 1842-1910.

found in the Lerwick Marriage Register.[26] Or it could suggest an action in the Sheriff Court.[27] Often, however, the men went to sea, and no more is heard of them.

Rich women could however bypass their local kirk and take their cases direct to the Commissary Courts, which, though based on the pre-Reformation dioceses, came to deal with a variety of civil cases including breach of promise.[28] These cases, like those in the Sheriff Court, pitted one party against another. There were none in Shetland, so far as we know.

Jurisdiction passed from the Commissary Courts to the Sheriffs' Courts by an Act of Parliament (4 Geo. 4 c. 97) in 1823.[29] This was mentioned by the defender's agent in the first breach of promise case brought before it in May 1823.

From the date of citation in this action right up to the 22 of May last the Defender was altogether at a loss what to think of the action, for he was called to answer before your Lordship to a libel only competent before the Commissaries of Edinburgh, but it now appears that when the summons came to be called on the 15th, the Pursuer awakened from her dream, was surprised to find herself before your Lordship, and justly concerned that amendment of the libel was necessary to suit her new situation.[30]

The method of pleading in the Sheriff Court was different, and emendations had to be made to the original summons.[31]

Altogether 25 cases were brought in the Sheriff Court in Shetland between 1823 and 1900. Most cases were brought for damages alone,

26   CH 2/1072/3, 28 January 27, CH 2/1072/13, 7 November 1838 and CH 2/1072/13, 30 March 1865

27   CH 2/1072/13, 18 March 86, 30 September 86.

28   C. Sinclair, *Tracing Scottish Local History: a Guide to Local History Sources in the Scottish Record Office*, (Scottish Record Office, HMSO, Edinburgh 1994)pp. 60-1.

29   It seems possible that the Sheriff Court in Shetland was precipitate in taking over the jurisdiction from the Comissary Court. See J.D. Wilson, *The Practice of the Sheriff Courts of Scotland in Civil Causes*, 3rd edn., Edinburgh, Bell and Barfut, 1883), p. 46. Its introduction is given as 1824.

30   SC 12/6/1823/13/5.

31   SC 12/6/1823/13/1 and 3.

but about a third for aliment as well, and a handful in both cases were settled by compromise. Not all cases ran their full course. In some cases the defender did not put in an appearance, and in other cases the record is tantalizingly incomplete.

The women who brought cases in the Sheriff Court were, with only two exceptions, country women. This is not immediately obvious, but it became clear in reading their petitions that they must come into Lerwick to prosecute their cases, and their petitions were made out as if they lived there. But it is not only clear that they really came from the country, but the men who jilted them lived nearby, usually in the same parish. Given the Shetland climate this is not unexpected. Country courtships could only be pursued on the long winter nights if a man's ardour could make light of long walks in foul weather, so that the distance between their homes set limits. Only one couple lived any distance from each other. In an 1883 case Charles James Spence lived on Unst, and Lillias Hay at Scatster on the Mainland, not far from Sullom Voe.[32] Their names suggest they were minor members of well-known local families. We do not know her occupation, but he was a fisherman, according to the 1881 census.

It is surprising that so small a proportion of the jilted women were Lerwick girls, even though the proportion of the population of Shetland living there was much smaller than it is now. Perhaps the Kirk in Lerwick was active enough in its war against sin to deal with most of its own cases. Or were country girls more naïve and trusting, but also more feisty? Perhaps we will be able to come to some conclusions when we have examined these cases in more detail.

The Progress of a Case

It will be useful however at this stage to look at the procedure of the Sheriff Court, which was much the same for all civil cases. Nevertheless procedure varied slightly. But by the 1880's cases had

32   Shetland Archives SC 12/6/1883/4.

become firmly structured, and Dove Wilson's *Practice of the Sheriff's Courts of Scotland* provides a useful guide from then to 1900 and beyond.[33] It is also helpful because it enunciates the principles which guided the court, even in the earlier period, so that it is possible to see when one looks at cases why procedures needed tightening up. I have used it extensively.

The Sheriff Court was presided over by the Sheriff-Substitute, commonly called the Sheriff. He was originally appointed by the Sheriff of the county, or of two neighbouring counties like Shetland and Orkney. This depended largely on size. To him the Sheriff-substitute sent appeals when problems arose in the Sheriff Court. The procedure used here for breach of promise cases was that in use for all cases under its jurisdiction.

The case always opened with a document called a Summons, or later a Petition. This stated the names of the pursuer (plaintiff in England) and the defender, their place of residence and their occupation. The document, which was drawn up by the pursuer's agent, then stated the amount of damages and *solatium* craved. Damages were seen as compensation for monetary loss and loss of 'market'; that is expectation. *Solatium* was for loss of character, prospects and hurt feelings. Perhaps because they were intimately connected they were never assessed separately. The sums asked for were never exceeded, rarely equalled, and usually considerably less.

If she had been seduced and the defender had fathered a child she could ask for lying-in expenses and aliment (maintenance for the child). Actual sums of money had to be explicitly stated. She would also ask for expenses, and the pursuer would pray to be granted 'a warrant to arrest upon the dependence', or 'fence' (i.e. freeze) his assets.

---

33   J.D.Wilson, *The Practice of the Sheriff Courts of Scotland, in Civil Causes*, (Bell and Bradfute, Edinburgh), pp. 101-194, 216. A useful legal dictionary is *Glossary: Scottish Legal Terms*, (Law Society of Scotland, Butterworths, Edinburgh, 1992.)

The next sections of the petition were the condescendence and the note of pleas at law. The first was or should be, an unemotional statement of the relevant facts on which the case was based. Early on it seems to have been a struggle to produce an acceptable condescendence. In the first group of cases the condescendence was separate from the summons of the pursuer, and those of both parties were the outcome of revisions of the defence and a reply by the pursuer.[34] The note might also be merged with it. It simply stated what was the legal basis of the case, that it was a valid case, and the sums craved were reasonable.

A copy of this document was sent to the defender, who sometimes made himself scarce. If so, it was left at his house with a relative, or, according to Dove Wilson, stuffed in the keyhole. I have yet to find a case of a keyhole used as a letterbox. If he intended to fight the case, the defender was required to reply in six days if he lived on the mainland, otherwise 14 days. Delays were often caused in the earlier part of the century through difficulties of travel in bad weather. As transport improved this became less of a difficulty. If the defender intended to fight the case he sent in a notice of appearance, and in due course his agent submitted his defence to the court. It should deal with each point raised in the condescendence and pleas at law in as factual and unemotional fashion as the pursuer. He might deny her averments in totality or in part, or state ameliorating circumstances, such as the behaviour of the pursuer. All the matters to be considered by the judge should have been set out in the condescendence of each party.

Each stage of the proceedings was minuted, along with any interlocutors, which provide at the least a guide to the order of events, and give interlocutors in full. An Interlocutor is 'the official and effective expressions of an order of judgement pronounced by the court in the course of a civil case.'[35] A note would be added to explain the

---

34   For example SC 12/6/1826/32/3
35   *Glossary*

rationale of any decision made by the Sheriff. Notes occurred during cases, and also embodied the final judgement.

All cases were minuted. The pursuer's petition and the defender's defence were now considered carefully, and the record was revised and adjusted. At this point the pursuer corrected or amplified points in her petition and replied to any of his averments. Now, if not earlier, letters and other relevant materials such as bills were produced and examined by the agents of each party. The record was then declared to be 'closed', and a date was set for the parties to prove their averments.

Witnesses were called. Now ordinary men and women appeared in open court and were subject to examination and cross-examination. Apart from letters this is as near as we get to hearing the voices of humble people. But most of them spoke in dialect, and their words are rendered in suspiciously good English. Nevertheless their attitudes survive, gossip surfaces, customs reveal themselves. From 1872 reports of court proceedings appeared in *The Shetland Times* and later *The Shetland News* and the letter columns of the papers may also contain comment. Both sources add further dimensions.

After the witnesses were heard a debate followed in court between the agents of each party making points to support or destroy the other party's case. They could be very lively, and the Sheriff's interjections played their part. These interchanges leave the impression that these members of the bar were all friends, a coterie even within Shetland's small professional class. They spoke the same language and enjoyed this legal jousting. These exchanges, though reported in the newspapers do not appear in the court's processes.

The judge now made avizandum (considered the case) and gave his final judgement or decree in an interlocutor, which appeared in the minutes and interlocutors, and in the local papers. The loser was ordered to pay the legal expenses of both parties, and the judge rounded off the case with a 'note' explaining the rationale of the case. Cases were heard without a jury. An appeal might be lodged against the level of the expenses of the case to the sheriff-in-chief, and if unsuccessful these merely increased expenses, which probably already exceeded any damages which had been awarded. The last item in the process consists of the expenses of each party.

Chapter 2

The First Cases (1823-1828)

The first breach of promise case in the Shetland Sheriff Court was brought in May 1823 by Isabella Halcrow, a servant to a small farmer in Whiteness, against James Davidson, a dyke-builder of Hoore, Whiteness.[36] The point was made that this was the first case of this sort in this court, by the defender's agent, who pointed out that the pursuer had at first assumed the case would be heard by the Commissary Court, and, indeed, Stout's case for Isabella quoted throughout precedents from that court. But in many ways the case showed a good deal of confusion. The court had jumped the gun for though the act transferring jurisdiction had been passed in 1823, it only came into effect in 1824.[37] At this time the training of Shetland's lawyers seems to have been done by serving an apprenticeship with another lawyer. There is no evidence that the pursuer's agent, William Stout, William Sievwright the defender's agent, or Andrew Duncan, the Sheriff Substitute were Edinburgh trained. Perhaps too, as such cases were rare in Shetland, failure to make use of precedents may have played a part.[38]

The procedure is generally confused and confusing. There seems to have been a problem in getting the pursuer's agent to deliver anything like a condescendence. Isabella was vague and Stout set out to impress with his learning and high-flown rhetoric. It was an object lesson in how

36   SC 12/6/1823/13.
37   4 Geo. IV c. 97.
38   I owe the former suggestion to Angus Johnson and the latter to Brian Smith, both of the Shetland Archives. See also M. S. Robertson, *Sons and Daughters of Shetland, 1800-1900*, (Shetland Publishing Company, 1991), pp. 198-9, 173, 36.

to lose a case. We shall follow in some detail these early cases, which provide such an excellent introduction to much of the life and attitudes of the period in Shetland, to say nothing of the problems of the Sheriff Court.

Isabella had become acquainted with James a considerable time before the case came to court, and he had gained her affections by his frequent expressions of esteem and love. She had accepted his proposal of marriage, and with his flattery he had led her astray. He robbed her of her innocence and 'the consequence of which criminal assignation was the procreation of a male child' (The language of the court was always excessively Latinate). James had acknowledged his paternity, and made arrangements for the nuptials. Then he stopped visiting her 'and left her the victim of his duplicity to starve with her infant and lament that unhappy situation into which she had been brought solely by his artifice.' She appealed to him to marry her, but he refused. He should therefore pay her £50 damages and solatium.[39] It was the sad story repeated, in case after case. They differ in detail. She failed to ask for aliment and lying-in expenses, but remedied her omission ten days later, when she asked for £3 aliment for her child to the age of seven, inlying expenses, and the expenses of the action.

William Sievwright put James' defence, starting by attacking Isabella's demand for damages. It was 'an extravagant feature of this extravagant case'. In the whole of their lives they would never possess £50 of free money. As a small farmer's servant she would earn no more than 10s to 12s in half a year, and he from 1s 6d to 2s a week. A sarcastic tone pervades Seivwright's analysis of the pursuer's case. 'Here is a painting for your Lordship, a kind of flourish upon the political picture drawn in the first two pages of the case'. But he cannot deny that intercourse took place. But since the child's birth he had paid £3 12s 7gd, including 2s 6d to the midwife, and he was willing to pay the

---

39   SC 12/6/1823/13/1.

proportion of upkeep for the child which the law demanded. The pursuer's conduct in raising an action was unnecessary and reprehensible.[40]

Isabella's answer, provided by Stout, was disdainful. The defender did not deny the facts of the case. She claimed her own case is unanswerable, but out of respect for the Sheriff replied. The law could provide redress for the 'calamities' she had suffered. Here Stout quoted the great legal authorities of the past, Stair and Erskine, on the need for reparation for damages, and then quoted precedents at length. In intercourse of this sort, he continued, the man was the more guilty party, but it was the woman who suffered irretrievable loss of reputation, and therefore could not obtain an honest living. The authors of these evils should be compelled to place the parties on a more equal footing. Poverty, prostitution and infamy were the consequences of similar crimes which were instanced by characters such as the defender had proved to be. 'Else why, it may be asked, are our streets and lanes (but a few years ago the resort of honest industry and female innocence) contaminated by the very shadow of such prostitutes?' Stout now descended from oratory to speak dismissively of the 'trifling articles' James had given Isabella for the child. James was not as poor as he made out.[41]

In his reply Sievwright, on James' behalf, took to pieces Isabella's agent's answers. He denied there had been any seduction or breach of promise, and though he had agreed to support the child, had hoped there would be no grounds for litigation. She had not proved the seduction, but has carried on through ten pages a most pompous and useless discussion of the point whether reparation was due when a wrong had been done. Sievwright, who was the most clued up of the lawyers, suggested that she be required to make an 'articulated' condescendence.[42] Duncan ordered her to do so.

---

40   SC 12/6/1823/13/5
41   SC 12/6/1823/13/7.
42   SC 12/6/1823/13/8; the points of an articulated condescendence were numbered.

In the beginning of her condescendence (whose numbering it would be tedious to follow) Isabella began by pointing out that at the beginning of a courtship a promise of marriage, though understood is a secret between the couple. She then gave details of the progress of their courtship, which was according to the practice of the country. She became pregnant and it was universally believed by the neighbours to have been on terms of marriage. Though her employers wished her to stay on, James had moved her into lodgings for which he had not paid, despite his assurances. He visited her, and told people he was determined to marry her. As for the advances he made to her for her confinement, he had systematically understated them to the court.[43]

James' answers were also numbered. It was pointed out that James and Isabella had lived next door to each other, and of necessity met frequently. The neighbours had no right to assume there was any promise of marriage. He did not deny the connection he had with her was morally wrong, but he never deceived her. There had been no need for her to move into lodgings so long as she could continue to work. As he could not prove the child was not his, though he believed this to be the case, he felt bound to support her to some extent. But it was wrong to deduce from this that such a seduction as his made him liable for damages. If this were so 'it would in fact be offering a premium to incontinency.' The first aim of the woman would be to inveigle the man into marriage, and if she failed in this she was to be rewarded with a 'dowry'.[44]

Duncan, the Sheriff, was not impressed by Isabella's proof. Her allegations in the condescendence, though relevant, were much too vague and general to support the gravity of the charge. James was assoilzied (absolved from) the claim for damages; but he was held liable for £3 aliment and 15s inlying expenses, minus what he had already

---

43   SC 12/6/1823/13/9
44   SC 12/6/1823/13/10.

paid. James must pay for extracting the decree, but no more.[45] Isabella had not gained the £50 she had asked for in damages, but though she had been granted aliment, she had to pay the expenses of her own action.[46]

It is difficult to imagine how she was regarded by those who knew her. Was she disgraced, so that she moved away from anywhere she was known? But it has been impossible to trace her any further. Her surname is a common one, which always makes a unique identification difficult. For all we know she married someone else.

The Fiddler and the Virago

The struggle to get a proper condescendence continued to be a problem in the next two cases, both brought in 1826. In the first of these the pursuer was accused by the Defender of having a fierce temper, but he appears not to have been much better. They seem to have enjoyed slanging matches. Some of these cases are tragic, but this one is a tragic-comedy. Later events will show that neither party suffered long.

When Margaret Mouat of Colvadale on Unst brought a case against William Nisbet, junior of Burrafirth, Unst on the 4th of April, 1826, she did not employ the pompous William Stout as her agent as Isabella had done three years earlier. She employed James Greig, the Procurator Fiscal. The summons provided a pathetic picture of a woman betrayed. It would appear that Greig, having listened to her story, had presented a sanitized version in his summons. Margaret was, she claimed, a respectable young woman, and quite well off. Though others had courted her she had no need to marry. She accepted William Nisbet because his professions of love and constancy appealed to her, and she agreed to marry him. After a courtship of nearly three years they agreed

45   An extract decree is a formal statement of the final judgement of the court which is obtained for enforcement.
46   SP 12/6/1823/13/10, The Sheriff's Interlocutor and Note were appended to this document. This was not the practice later.

The Fiddler and the Virago

to marry at the beginning of December last. William gained her father's consent. Spirits and other articles for an immediate wedding were bought; but William, without any cause, abandoned her, and refused to marry her. 'He had inflicted irreparable injury on her, by breaking her fortune and peace of mind, and indelibly wounding her feelings.' He should pay her £100 damages and solatium, and pay the expenses of the case, and his goods, gear etc. remain under sure fence until sufficient cation (surety) was found.[47]

The summons was transmitted to William and a day appointed to hear his defence. Margaret seems to have replied to his defence with such intemperate language that Sheriff Duncan ordered that her reply be withdrawn and reframed in more moderate terms. As for William's defences, framed by William Sievwright, which had aroused her ire, Duncan had 'not been able to discover anything objectionable in the defences bating some argument which strictly speaking perhaps ought to have been omitted.'[48] This was on the second of November, 1826. Margaret appealed to the Sheriff Principal in Edinburgh. He considered William's defence and Margaret's reply together with Margaret's appeal. He furiously scored out nine-tenths of Margaret's appeal.[49] He confirmed Duncan's verdict on Margaret's reply, but overturned that on William's defence. None of them were in regular form. As a result both defence and reply were removed from the record, and only Margaret's appeal remains. Duncan recorded the verdict from Edinburgh, which overturned his decision on William's defence and appointed new days for the revised defence and reply to be heard.[50] These reveal an entirely different picture.

According to William he had been acquainted with Margaret for some time.[51] Probably Margaret was right about dates. Anyway, some

47   SC/12/6/1826/32/1. On Greig see Robertson, p. 64.
48   SC12/6/1826/32/3
49   SC 12/6/1826/32/5.
50   SC 13/6/1826/32/3.
51   SC 12/6/1826/32/4.

time later he made proposals over marriage 'and as might be supposed, although he does not know that he – as she or some one for her now chooses to express it – expressed himself in terms of admiration – he paid her such attentions as are usual on such occasions and such as might be expected from persons of his rank and education'.[52] The fact that the language of the pursuer's and defender's statements was due to their agents wording is made clear here. The rather coy rendering of William's description of country courtship must be Sievwright's, made in language palatable to middle class Shetland sensibilities. He knew nothing about other admirers, but he admitted she consented to become his wife, and when he returned from the Davis Straits about Martinmas 1825 they agreed to marry about Christmas. It was not his fault they did not marry then. He gained her father's consent and every arrangement was made for the wedding. He did not, as the Pursuer wrote it, without cause abandon her and neglect to solemnize his marriage with her. He did not marry her after she refused him for the following reasons, which induced him to declare he would never marry her. Her violent and overbearing temper worried him, and the nearer the time for the wedding approached, the more obvious this disposition became. When he had been at the fishing, and also at home, he had practised the violin. After his return in 1825 Mr Ingram, the minister of his parish, was some time absent from the Island, and he attended the Independent Meeting House with some satisfaction. When Margaret heard this she upbraided him in front of her sister and friends and told him that she had heard that under its influence he had given up the violin. She would 'turn him off' if he intended to follow such a Society. Although he saw it was an attempt to 'try on the breeches' he continued to visit her and went to town to buy things for their wedding. He bought her, besides sugar, tea and spirits etc, 40s to 50s worth of dresses, which she still retained. But

---

52   SC 12/6/1826/32/4.

now, he could not imagine why, she upbraided him for 'drunkenness and whoredom' whilst he was in Lerwick. Christmas arrived, but not Mr Ingram. However, various marriage parties were going over to Fetlar to be married, and he suggested they should join one of the parties the next week and make the crossing. He advised Margaret and her family of his plan and asked what day would suit them before the weekend. They utterly refused. They would wait for Mr Ingram's return. He was forced to conclude that this was either a further display of her 'wilful and unbending obstinacy of which he had already had too much occasion to observe and lament', or she was looking for an excuse to break off the match. He came to believe that even if she still loved him there was little hope of happiness in such a marriage, and he should break off all communication with her. She sent for him 'to speak with him' but he did not go and at length her father came to him and said that if they could not agree 'in God's name to part in peace.' Further, he regretted ever having supported his daughter in her refusal to go to Fetlar. William said he would never marry her, and could not be compelled to do so by law. He added, as further proof of her 'benevolent disposition' she had been using every possible means to prevent him from earning something that summer to support himself or pay the damages she demanded. The breach was not on his part, and he was entitled to withdraw from it free from blame, and there could be no claim against him for the expense of the wedding, as he had paid for everything.[53]

Margaret's reply was much briefer than his: seven pages to his nineteen, for they simply amounted to a flat denial of his defence, save where it agreed with the statements in her summons.[54] Duncan at last ordered them each to give in a condescendence in regular form. Neither of them did so, and the case ended inconclusively.[55]

---

53   Ibid.
54   SC 12/6/1826/32/6.
55   SC 12/6/1826/32/3.

Fond Hopes Destroyed

More is known of the history of Margaret and William thanks to the research of May Sutherland the Unst local historian.[56] Margaret, who seems to have been something of a belle, married in 1829 and had five children. Only one other woman in a breach of promise case is known to have married. William, on the other hand, was one of at least nine men who married. Demography and the double standard blighted the women's marital prospects.

An Ageist has his Fingers Burnt

Sievwright was an able and successful lawyer. Elizabeth Donaldson of Hamnavoe, Yell, probably saw him as the right man to bring her case against Sinclair Gilbertson of Ulsta, also in Yell. In the summons, dated 28 May, 1826 Sievewright painted the usual picture of a woman betrayed.[57] Elizabeth, or Betty, as she was probably known, had been courted for some years previously, and on the 20th of February 1824, a Saturday, Sinclair gained her consent to marry him. He stayed overnight with her and the next day returned to his home and sent his brother to the Precentor asking him to read the banns that day. They returned to Hamnavoe for the Contract, which was attended by 20 neighbours and friends. The wedding was arranged for the Tuesday of the week following, that is, the week after the next. Sinclair returned to Elizabeth's house and stayed with her until the Tuesday, when they invited their friends and relations to the wedding. They then went to his parents' house to invite them, and stayed there until the Thursday, and he then accompanied her part of the way back to Hamnavoe, still resolved to marry her on the fixed day. She laid in supplies from the shop at Burravoe, and put her house in order. But on the next day, the Friday, he sent a boy to her house to say he did not intend to marry her. He gave no reason, but asked her to return him a shirt and hat, which he had left at her house and were part of his marriage suit of clothes. By

56   Letter to Angus Johnson, Shetland Archives, 26 July 2001
57   SC 12/6/1826/45/1.

An Ageist has his fingers Burnt

his unworthy and degrading conduct he had not only 'outraged her feelings and destroyed her peace of mind, but she had been held up as a spectacle to the parish and her character and respectability sacrificed by him'. He had violated his solemn vows and was now liable to make proper reparation. Therefore he should pay her £50.

During the case Elizabeth must frequently have thought of that strange case at Vigon in North Yell only three years earlier, with roles reversed, for news of it would have spread through Yell like wildfire. She was made of sterner stuff than Charles Rusland.

Sinclair's defence, which was in the hands of James Greig, was brutally brief. He was a poor inexperienced young man, aged between 20 and 30, known to be 'of a facile disposition and imbecile mind', while she was a rich old woman of 53. It was she who had pressed marriage on him. To marry her would have been misery for both of them, so that considering their happiness he abandoned all idea of marrying her. She had suffered no injury or pecuniary loss, and it could not be believed that a woman of so advanced an age, could have suffered any 'heart distress' or shock to her feelings. He was fully entitled to resile from such a preposterous engagement. As he was 'a poor lad, not worth £5 in the world', he hoped the Sheriff would not award damages against him.[58]

Sievwright on Elizabeth's behalf went on the attack in his reply.[59] Sinclair's conduct belied his claim to facility and imbecility. When Sinclair Gilbertson had visited Lerwick to consult his agent he had taken him in and misled him. Whether she was 53 or 43, experienced or the reverse, rich or poor, did not excuse his behaviour. She had never coaxed him into a promise of marriage. And it was quite false that she had never suffered any pecuniary loss. When her summons reached him he renewed his protestations of his regard for her, regretted he had followed the advice of his friends 'and carried matters again so far' that she had again purchased stores from Mr Leisk at Burravoe and

58   SC 12/6/1826/45/4
59   SC 12/6/1826/45/4

authorised him to write to her agent to stop the proceedings.[60] He now felt safe enough to bid her goodbye. She now had no doubt the Sheriff would teach him it was not so easy to sport with the feelings of his fellow creatures and award her damages commensurate with the wrong he had done her.

The Sheriff now ordered both parties to hand in condescendences. Elizabeth handed in a factual document framed in line with the terms of her summons. Greig stated that his client did not intend to give in a condescendence. Duncan now made avizandum and, apparently taking a hint from Sinclair's reply, awarded Elizabeth the very sum mentioned there – £5 – and, of course, the expenses of the case.[61]

According to the Mid and South Yell Marriage register a Sinclair Gilberton was married at Lussetter in August 1827, just over seven months after the end of the case. What happened to Elizabeth is uncertain. Perhaps she was the Betty Donaldson, listed in the 1841 Census of Burravoe as a domestic servant aged 66. The age would fit well enough, but she must have suffered a decline in status and wealth.

Poor Barbara at Law

The next case has similarities to the case Isabella Halcrow of Whiteness brought against James Davidson in 1823.[62] In 1828 Barbara Smith brought a case against James Tait. Both Barbara and James came from Tingwall, shared the same parish minister as the inhabitants of Whiteness, and they all probably attended the Tingwall Kirk.[63] Barbara, Isabella and James were all servants. Like Isabella, Barbara brought a case for aliment as well as damages. However, Barbara differed in applying to be put on the Poor's Roll, very probably on the advice of her minister, Mr Turnbull.

---

60   SC 12/6/1826/45/6
61   SC 12/6/1826/45/7; SC 12/6/1826/45/3
62   See above, SC 12/6/1823/13
63   On Turnbull see Robertson, p. 217.

Barbara's agent was William Sievwright, and her summons tells the usual story of the maiden betrayed. She had been seduced by his fair promises and in an unlucky moment had submitted to his embraces, and the consequence was she became pregnant. A wedding day was fixed for Martinmas last, and he spoke about it freely, and apparently with determination. But as the date approached he found reasons for delay. It was fixed for Candlemas and then Whitsuntide, but both came and went, and in the meantime because of her weak state of pregnancy she had to leave service without any means of support. The child was born on the twenty-ninth of April and was the son of James Tait. He refused to marry her or provide for the child, and was well aware she could not provide for it. He should be made to pay her £30 damages, 30s inlying expenses and 50s aliment yearly until the child was seven, plus the expenses of the case.[64]

The summons was dated 26th May 1828, and James was cited on the twenty-sixth. He was to appear before the Sheriff on the fifth of June.[65] In a perfect funk he rushed over to see Mr Turnbull on the third of June to ask him for a certificate to be put on the Poor's Roll. Sometime in July Andrew Duncan (the son of the Sheriff), as his agent, presented his petition. Probably at this point Mr Turnbull may have tipped Barbara that she should put in an application herself. Her own certificate from Turnbull was dated the fifteenth of July, and Sievwright submitted her certificate and petition on the 14th of August.[66] It was remitted to the agent of the poor, Gilbert Duncan (the Sheriff's brother) by Sievwright, and on the 7th of October he was appointed to conduct the case.[67] The matter of the petitions having been settled in Barbara's favour, the breach of promise case was resumed, and James' defence was presented at last in late November by his agent.[68] As James had been refused the benefit of the Poor's Roll because he had admitted that

64   SC 12/6/1828/85/1
65   SC 12/6/1828/85/2
66   SC 12/6/1828/85/13 and Sc 12/6/1828/85/12
67   SC 12/6/1828/85/6 and SC 12/6/1828/85/12
68   SC 12/6/1828/85/3 and SC 12/6/1828/85/4

he had 'connection' with the pursuer seven months before the birth of the child, and so being unable to afford a defence, he was reduced to a state of extreme wretchedness. He did not believe he was the father of the child, and he was entitled to demand the pursuer take an oath before the proof of his paternity was settled.[69]

In the reply Sievewright made on her behalf, Barbara expressed her willingness to take an oath declaring James was the father of her child. As for the question of breach of promise, James had produced no defence. In replying to the summons he was required by law to admit or deny the facts stated in it.[70] But he had directed his defence only to matters of aliment, and said nothing about damages. She was ready to take the oath, and should be awarded both aliment and damages.[71]

She took the oath in mid-December, and before Christmas the judge awarded her 40s aliment instead of the 50s she had asked for, 15s instead of the 30s inlying expenses and £1 instead of the £30 damages and *solatium* she had craved. Judges often took a person's circumstances into consideration in such cases, but this was simply an expression of contempt.[72] It was enough to put any woman off bringing a case. If so its effects were remarkably long lasting.

69   SC 12/6/1828/85/8
70   6 Geo. IV. c. 120
71   SC 12/6/1828/85/7; SC 12/6/1828/85/3
72   SC 12/6/1628/85/3

Chapter 3

Two Feisty Females

After 1828 there were no more cases of breach of promise with or without aliment for thirty-nine years, then in seven years there were seven cases, none involving aliment. There seems no obvious reason for this, and I do not intend to be diverted into fields where I have no competence whatever. It may be that for a variety of reasons women were becoming more self-confident. Certainly the first three cases were all brought in early 1867. Two came from Fetlar and one from Papa Stour. The women may have met in Lerwick, found they had all been let down by faithless lovers, and one determining on bringing a case, the others followed suit. One of the women seems to have lost her nerve and withdrawn the case the day she brought it, so that there is a summons and a bill for the expenses of the case for her to pay.[73]

Whereas in the earlier period none of the cases involved witnesses, these cases are remarkable for the number of witnesses who were called. This was the result of introducing a new short form of record.[74] The summons was abbreviated. It gave the names, occupations and places of residence of pursuer and defender as formerly, and then stated that the defender should pay so much in damages and solatium as he had courted the woman for a named period of time and promised to marry her, and now had failed to do so. The defender then replies almost as briefly, either denying the charge or saying that she had not suffered greatly, and that the damages claimed were excessive. The whole

73   SC 12/6/1867/3
74   SC 12/6/1867/2

33

business of finding out the reason why the courtship had failed, which had been sorted out in the summons, the defence and the condescendence were lost, and the judge had to depend entirely on the evidence of witnesses and the skill of their agents in examining them to come to a conclusion.

The Fetlar Girl and the Faithless Sailor

The first of the three, Catharine Affleck of Lerwick, brought her case against James Johnson of Fetlar on the 4th of January, 1867. She demanded £60 damages with interest until the sum was paid. There were delays in James responding as the weather was bad and this caused delays. He was fined, and in the wrangle over its imposition Catharine became even more bloody-minded. At last, on the 7th of February he appeared and denied that there had been any breach of promise, or any grounds for the action. Further the damages claimed were excessive, and he was a poor man.[75]

On the 14th of February Catharine handed in six letters James had written to her from Leith, New Zealand and Sydney, to be used in evidence. The evidence was going to be heard in the Court Room at Fort Charlotte on the 21st of February, but the defender's agent, John William Spence was taken ill, and the evidence only started to be presented on the 30th of March. James gave evidence first.[76] He had been courting her in 1858, and he had been out of the country twice since then. They had been sweethearting but he had never said anything about marrying. He had never said he would give her his 'write'. When he was asked if he referred to marrying her when he wrote 'I told you that I would not have another than you', he agreed that he did, both there and in several other letters. He had not written 'My mind is the same as ever'. Did he mean he would marry her when he came home?

75   SC 12/6/1867/2/1
76   SC 12/6/1867/2/18, pp. 1-8

The Fetlar Girl and the Faithless Sailor

He replied that he meant that so long as he wrote to his parents he would write to her. He had returned to Fetlar the last time in July 1866, and saw her three times after that. He denied that he had said to her that he would like to marry her in the house of her brother-in-law, George Donaldson, or that he had come home to marry her. He had brought her home a piece of gold to make her a ring, but it was not intended as a wedding ring. At the last interview he had with her he did not say 'What can part us now, and he did not remember her replying 'Perhaps the first lie you may hear': and he did not reply, 'No, nothing unless one of us be shot'. A lot must have gone on behind the scenes not to be found in the court processes. Before he was handed over for cross-examination by Samuel Henry, Catharine's agent, he said that that night he had stayed from ten at night until four in the morning. He told Henry that he had left home in 1858 and given up courting her. Was this, Henry asked, because he had heard of her improper conduct? This question was objected to by Spence, as it had not been mentioned in James' minute of defence, and the objection was over-ruled.[77] James told the court that he had given up courting her because he had heard another lad was. He had written her accordingly, and on his return to Fetlar in 1861 only spoke to her as to anyone else. After he left home in April 1861 they became friendlier. He was away until July 1866, and he wrote quite a number of letters to her during this time, and intended to marry her, but never told her so in words. On his return though he heard from two women of her improper conduct on the peat hill at Fetlar.

Re-examined by his own agent he said he had recommenced courting her in 1859 because he had never really believed the reports he had heard of her. In the last interview he had with her he mentioned a report a lad was courting her. He had never been told she had refused another lad. He discontinued his engagement, and told her brother, George Donaldson 'he had heard enough to be disgusted', for he had heard she was sweethearting another. He did not question Catharine

77   SC 12/6/1867/2/1; SC 12/6/1867/2/3, pp. 9-10; Robertson, p. 79

whilst they were on Fetlar, for if she had jilted him he did not think it worthwhile to enquire into her affairs. 'My only reason for not marrying her was the report of the two women.'[78]

Catharine now gave evidence contradicting much of his.[79] He had courted her from 1858 to 1866. In 1861 before going abroad he had said they were to live with his father after marriage. The letters she had produced were from him, and she had many more. On his return in 1866 he had visited her on the Thursday and the Saturday, and he stayed overnight on both occasions and they discussed arrangements for the marriage – but not in bed with her. She said she would like to marry at her brother-in-law's house, as they were leaving at Hallowmas. He brought her a piece of gold he had meant of course for a wedding ring. When he was there on the Saturday night she told him of the report that another had been courting her, and she said it was untrue. He said what did he care, she was here and that was all he wanted. But for her engagement she could have been married to others. The last time he visited her he had said, on leaving, 'What can separate us now?' and she had answered, 'Perhaps the first lie they would tell him', to which he replied, 'No, nothing can part us, unless one of us be shot'. He never called again, and did not reply to her messages, until she sent her brother-in-law, and received the answer that 'if he married me at night he would leave me in the morning'. She fainted and went into a swoon. He did not reply to her letter asking his reason, and she left Fetlar at Hallowmas.

Henry now cross-examined her about her other sweethearts. Before 1861 she had been courted by another man, as she had been freed to do so by a letter from James. There had been a certain Andrew Tait, a sailor, before 1861, but she did not know his address. When asked the names of others she demurred, then admitted they were not exactly offers of marriage, but might have been so. No one had been on courting

78   SC 12/6/1867/2/18, pp. 1-8
79   SC 12/6/1867/2/18, pp. 8-13

terms since then. Yes, she knew James Andrew Laurenson, but they had not been courting before 1867. He visited her, but he had only stayed late with her once, when he came with another lad and her sister had put him out. He often came and sat down in the house like any other person. It was the custom of the country to sit late. She was then asked if Laurenson had slept with her in the little house on the hill one night. 'No thank you, sir.' There were no beds or bedding on the hill, and she never slept there. Was she ever before the Kirk Session of Fetlar for improper conduct. 'No, Sir, I was not.'

Re-examined, she said she had asked the defender to explain his conduct. She had wanted to vindicate her character, and wanted to know who had said she was brought before the Kirk Session. She could get certificates of good behaviour. This concluded her evidence, and like most of the other women who were witnesses in this case, she did not append her signature. She said she could not write.[80] If she did not lie, she must have used an amanuensis to write her letters to James. We shall come across another case where an amanuensis was used.

James now produced five witnesses in his support, including women who had been at the peat cutting, and the youths who had visited Catharine at night. In her turn Catharine produced three witnesses to support her case. The examination of these witnesses sought to test and amplify the evidence given by James and Catharine and much of it was repetitive. Andrew Mure summed up, and awarded damages. He found that James had courted Catharine and had promised to marry her. On his return some women had brought him reports of improprieties on her part, and he forsook her without making enquiries into their truth. No immorality was proved against her, and there was nothing to justify his conduct towards her. He awarded her £25 damages and the expenses of the case which came to almost £15.[81]

---

80   SC 12/6/1867/2/18, pp. 13-38. The only women to sign their depositions were two of James' rumour-mongering witnesses.
81   SC 12/6/1867/2/18, pp.12-3

In the note appended to his judgement something of its rationale becomes clear. A strong effort had been made by the defender to prove impropriety, which had failed in his opinion. Both were natives of Fetlar, and the habits of the peasantry of that island, as perhaps of some other parts of Shetland and elsewhere here, are not so refined or correct as to be hoped they would in the course of time become. But the defender must have known all this, and it was thought he could not be justified in his conduct towards her, merely because she followed the customs of the place. He thought the most had been made of what had taken place, and the evidence when carefully examined reduced the facts to a small matter. 'The damages given are on the one hand not vindictive, nor on the other, merely nominal.'[82]

Strife on Papa Stour

There were similarities between this case and that of Catharine Affleck. Both women were involved with seamen, whose letters provided crucial evidence. The women treasured their letters. They lived at home and both were involved in the seasonal activities of their island communities. When they brought their cases they used the same newly introduced form of summons, which resulted in the evidence of witnesses becoming essential if sense was to be made of them. When Ann Jamieson brought her case against James Fraser she asked, like Catharine, for £50 damages. James Fraser's minute of defence presaged a hard fought case. He denied the whole grounds of the case, but claimed further, that if he had engaged to marry her 'she drew back; and gave him up and refused to marry him'[83]. He also caused endless delays.

Half way through this case, just after Ann Jamieson had given her evidence, it was disallowed. On the 24th of June, 1868, the Sheriff in Chief, writing from Edinburgh, dealing with the problems of James' delays, added a note drawing the Sheriff-Substitute's attention to an act

82   SC 12/6/1867/2/3, p. 13.
83   SC 12/6/1867/4/1.

of 1853 which, though, for the first time, made it possible for the parties to an action to be examined as witnesses in Scotland, yet expressly excluded actions for breach of promise of marriage, 'so that in reference to the present action the old law of Scotland is in full force'.[84] The evidence of the pursuer, which had been taken apparently without any objection by an oversight on the part of the defender's late agent, would have to be disregarded.[85] If the lawyers discussed its application to Catharine Affleck's case, to which it was also applicable, is not known.

Ann's evidence was to be ignored, and Fraser's was never taken. He produced three witnesses, including the Procurator Fiscal, and we have their evidence. His letters, however, also provide evidence of a sort. Ann lived a second and more exciting life through them, short and repetitive though most were. They had been courting from about Lammas 1859 (1 August)[86], and he wrote to her from Lerwick just before sailing on 1 March, 1860:

I am shipped to go to Greenland and from their to the Davy Streats so if God spairs my life I wont be til coming on to hallemis (1 November) so I hope you will be redy to Get mawred till I com hom and if God spairs my life I hop you will be redy till I com hom.[87]

God did spare his life, but only just, perhaps amused by this pious epistle. He was shipwrecked. He returned home having lost his clothes and in no condition to marry, according to Ann's evidence. He went off again down south to the herring fishing, and wrote with news of friends at the fishing, and requests for news from home.

You must writ me as sone as this comes to you and let me know how al is Going on you will Be having fine times leading the Peats.[88]

84   SC 12/6/1867/4/3; *Bell,* pp. 357-8; 16 Vict. c. 20
85   SC 12/6/1867/4/3. Samuel Henry, the defender's agent had died on 29th March 1868 (Robertson, p. 79). William Sievwright, Junior, took over the case (Robertson, p. 175).
86   SC12/6/1867/4/20, p.1
87   SC 12/6/1867/4/7
88   SC 12/6/1867/4/8

Fond Hopes Destroyed

This was in August 1860, but when he returned he was still 'in no condition to marry', so he went south to better himself and was away for three years. He wrote to her from Liverpool, Montreal, Shanghai and Hong Kong. His letters were as short as ever but he was avid for news from home, enquiring of friends, complaining that Ann had forgotten him, relieved when the mail caught up with him.

However, at last, in March 1863, he wrote of being home in the winter, and told her to 'Prepare your self for to Git Wed'. But there was clearly no rush, for he only returned on New Year's Day, 1864. He was 'still coming after me', according to Ann, but she had heard he was going with another. She confronted him, and he denied the charge. She believed him, 'for I did not think he could break his Vows'. But he came no more to their house. He made excuses and grew angry, and told her that he had heard that she had given his letters to friends to read and mock him, and that the letters were burnt. She fell to this bait, and told him it was not true, and that she could show him the letters. He came to the house at night when her mother and sisters were in bed, and the men at the fishing, and snatched the letters from her, and refused to return them.

Feeling a need of advice, she consulted the Session Clerk of Papa confidentially, and he approached Fraser, and Fraser said that if he had anything of hers she should come and get it. She then heard he was going away again, and she went to Lerwick to see the Procurator Fiscal, Mr. Duncan. Duncan had him arrested and brought to his office, and when he was confronted he admitted he had taken the letters.[89] It was two or three years after these events that Duncan was called on to give evidence for the Defence, and we now take up the story from his point of view.[90] He told how the Sheriff had examined Fraser, and concluded that in taking the letters he had done nothing criminal. The letters were

---

89   SC 12/6/1867/4/20, pp.1-5
90   SC 12/6/1867/4/20, p.5 and 13-15. Charles Gilbert Duncan, writer, was in 1868 chief magistrate. He was also much sought for advice, often given free. J.W. Irvine, *Lerwick, the birth and growth of an island town*, (Lerwick Community Council, 1985), pp.148-50; Robertson, pp. 36-7; information Brian Smith.

restored to the pursuer finally by Duncan, and Fraser said he was willing to marry her. Duncan had various conversations with them, attempting to reconcile them. 'There was a good deal of temper.' The man said he was ready to marry the woman before he went on his voyage, but she did not think that would be prudent. The upshot was that he wrote her a letter dated July 12th 1864.

> *Ann Jamieson*
> *I here by promise*
> *That I will marry you on*
> *My arivle home which will*
> *Bee about 8 months*
> *James Fraser* [91]

She said she would see if he stood by it. She thought the letter had been drawn from him by undue pressure, and she wanted him punished. Her feelings had been outraged. Marriage could do very little good under the circumstances, and she had been 'brought into the mouth of the public in the island where she lived.'[92]

According to Ann[93] he came to her lodgings after this interview and asked her to walk out with him, but her landlady would not let her go, as she feared he might do her violence. Fraser went South and did not return at the promised time. He returned at the Lammas just past (1 August 1866), and came into the house where she and her sister lived, and asked her to go out with him. He asked her again if she would marry him, and she said, 'yes, of course.' He asked if that were right, for they would be mocked, and he blamed her for the incident of the letters. He was very angry. He came to her again, when 'four of us girls', including her sister Helen, were burning a kelp kiln. He had George Eunson with him, and he asked her to walk with him. George and her sister followed. Again he blamed her. He did not love her, and he 'would see the fire she was burned in' [presumably in hell]. She replied (maddeningly) that she

91 SC 12/6/1867/4/19
92 SC 12/6/1867/4/20, pp. 13-15.
93 SC 12/6/1867/4/20, p. 6

was sorry for his evil heart if he could say so, because if she saw him burning she would try to deliver him, and she forgave him for all he had done. He did not forgive her. They did not speak again. 'He is married now. He married Anne Hughson in November last.'[94]

This evidence of Ann's was disallowed, and the case depended on the evidence of their witnesses. Helen was called first, and she essentially corroborated Ann's evidence. She had followed her sister together with George Eunson who was Fraser's closest friend. She did not like to leave her alone with Fraser. He had seized the letters about the time he married Anne Hughson. As for the conversation that night in August, neither she nor George could hear anything of it. Ann and Fraser never met again.[95]

George Eunson said he had overheard a conversation between Ann and Fraser on the 29th of September, when he had asked her if she was ready to marry him. She said she did not know. He said she could appoint a time, and she replied that she would not marry him 'except she liked'. He had not gone purposely to listen, as was put to him, and he did not have any other conversation with Fraser after this. Under cross-examination he corrected himself. Yes, he had, once, 'after the pursuer stopped the proclamation of the banns', Fraser asked me if I remembered that conversation. He told Fraser what he had overheard, and said he would be willing to testify in a Court of Justice.[96]

Peter Urquhart, the Lerwick police constable, also gave evidence for the defence. He had suggested to Fraser that the marriage might take place before he went away, and that would satisfy everyone, so they had called at Ann's lodgings to talk to her, and Fraser had said if she wished to marry him before he went away, she needed to make ready at once. She said 'No', and on being asked by the constable what she meant, she had replied that she meant that the last state might be worst than the

---

94   SC 12/6/1867/4/20, pp 6-10; Papa Stour Births deaths and Marriages Register, 13 Dec. 1866. The banns were probably read in November.
95   SC 12/6/1867/4/20, pp.10-12.
96   SC 12/6/1867/4/23

first. Fraser then asked her what she meant, but if she replied he did not remember what she said. He had had another conversation with Fraser before he went south. She said she would not have a present of him, and he had proof of that as he had another person listening that she did not know about.[97]

Sheriff Mure now considered all the evidence and analysed it carefully in a final note. The Defender's long series of letters in themselves showed there had been a promise of marriage. The Pursuer's sister had spoken of his change of feelings in 1864. However, the Defence had argued that the evidence of the Procurator Fiscal and the police constable showed that she had consented to dissolve the bond between the parties, but the Sheriff disagreed. After all that had happened she had reason to pause and consider how far the Defender's expressions of willingness to marry her were consistent with his feelings and behaviour. George Eunson's deposition was also inconsistent with the evidence of the Pursuer's sister and that of the policeman. 'That a special friend of the Defender's should come by accident upon the Pursuer and the Defender on a dark night and unseen by both overhear the former just in the act of refusing to honour her engagement is a very wonderful thing, and very unlikely to have happened.' And then soon after this alleged interview the Pursuer forbade the banns of the Defender and his wife. This showed that, rightly or wrongly, she considered him bound by his vows and she took the extreme step of claiming him for her own. This was inconsistent with her indignantly refusing to have anything to do with him.

There had been a breach of promise, and the Sheriff awarded her £25 in damages and *solatium* and the expenses which came to £13-10-10.[98]

97   SC 12/6/1867/4/20, pp. 15-16.
98   SC 12/6/1867/4/3 (unpaginated)

Chapter 4

Compromises (1870-1874)

T he next three Shetland cases in this period involved compromises. It almost looks as if some sort of grapevine was active: Shetland men were taking preventive action. There were considerable advantages for the defender if a case could be aborted and settled out of court. With luck it could prevent gossip and ill-will, and as lawyers could point out, though the pursuer would ask for a large sum, even though she was most unlikely to get what she asked for, if he could offer her a small sum in cash, she might be satisfied. It was a way of buying the girl off, applied at rather a late stage. A compromise would only work however, if the pursuer was prepared to forego the satisfaction of revenge, or if, on second thoughts she decided that a settlement out of court would save her reputation, but not, of course, if the defender offered too small a sum in compensation for her to cooperate. However none of these cases really worked out to the advantage of either party. The court remained in control.

The Culswick Case

Margaret Abernethy of Culswick entered a summons against Robert Mann, also of Culswick.[99] Culswick was an isolated community at the head of a voe on the Westside, some fifteen miles from Lerwick. The case was precipitated by Robert's marrying Joan Fraser, on 23rd

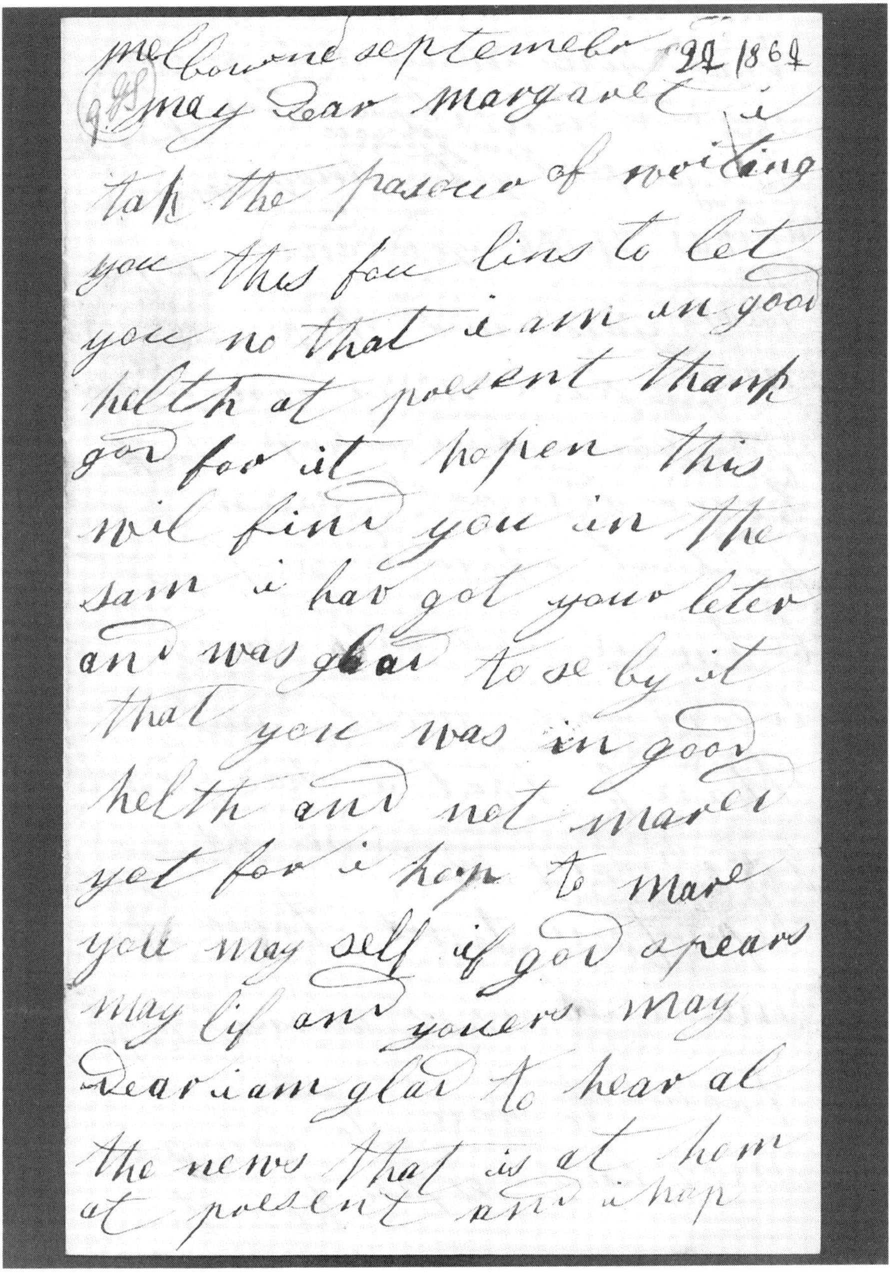

melbourne septemeber 24 1864
may dear margaret i
tak the pasour of writing
you this few lins to let
you no that i am in good
helth at present thank
god for it hopen this
wil find you in the
sam i hav got your leter
and was glad to se by it
that you was in good
helth and not maried
yet for i hop to mare
you may self if god spears
may lif and youers may
dear i am glad to hear al
the news that is at hom
at present and i hop

In hopes of marrying …

Fond Hopes Destroyed

December 1869 at Bridge of Walls.[100] Over the next month Margaret and her family became consumed with indignation, and Margaret braved the elements to consult a lawyer in Lerwick, and on January 21, 1870 she initiated her case, claiming £50 damages. The summons took four days to reach Robert at Culswick, and he put in a notice of appearance. The case was set to start on the 23rd of February, and it looked like being a straightforward case. Robert intended to deny there had been any promise of marriage. However, on the second of February Margaret deposited a series of Robert's letters with her lawyer. In turn he passed them on to Robert's lawyer, William Sievwright. The letters, written whilst Robert was abroad, were enough to destroy Robert's defence.[101]

100   The bride was 25, the groom 33. They were married by Rev. W. Rose, minister of Sandsting (Robertson, pp. 162-3).

101   SC 12/6/1870/4/24

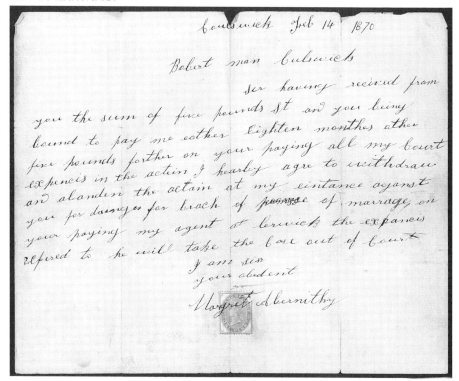

... and of compromising.

The Culswick Case

From Liverpool, as he set out on his travels he wrote that he hopes she will be as true to him as he to her.[102] From Melbourne, in 1863 he hoped she had not forgotten him, and hoped to be home soon: 'i would lik to be along sid of you and to hear ol your news.'[103] The crucial letter came through in August 1864, again from Melbourne: he was glad she was in good health 'and not mared yet, for I hop to mare you my self if god spears my life and youers May dear'.[104] He wrote his last letter from the gold diggings in Hokitika, New Zealand in 1868. 'I am gitin Tard of noken about the world bot do not like to be without Doing some Good for may self after som of the boys comen hom with lots of mone the peple woul think that i was spent som other way but if i should com with litel or non i hop that you wil not think so'.[105]

Sievwright saw Robert in Lerwick about the tenth of February and advised him to reach a compromise with Margaret.[106] It was still deep winter, and the last miles home were over a roadless waste. His feet were in a shocking condition, and he felt in no state to face Margaret.[107] But Joan, his wife, thought she could do it as well as he.[108]

On the 12th of February she went to see the woman she had ousted from Robert's affections, and 'in peace' suggested a compromise. Robert offered to pay £5 immediately and £5 more within eighteen months, and he would also pay the expenses of the process. Margaret wished to consult her parents overnight, and the next day, in the presence of her parents, she accepted the offer. As Margaret could not write Joan made out a receipt. Later Margaret was to argue that she had signed the receipt before it was read out to her and that she had been subject to fraud and misrepresentation, a view not accepted by the court. Perhaps Robert decided the case against him was really not very strong,

102   SC 12/6/1870/4/4
103   SC 12/6/1870/4/19
104   SC 12/6/1870/4/7
105   SC 12/6/1870/4/10
106   SC 12/6/1870/4/18
107   SC 12/6/1870/4/23/3
108   SC 12/6/1870/4/2, 23, pp. 12-15, 17-22

47

be that as may be, he offered if his money was returned, the action for damages could proceed. Margaret did not accept the offer. She rejected it, but nor did she repay the money. Therefore the compromise stood, and Robert paid over the second instalment to Margaret's lawyer.[109] The case dragged on into 1871 owing to their indecision and litigiousness and it was not until October 1871 that the accounts were settled. She got her expenses up to the date of the compromise, and the defender expenses for the remainder of the period.[110]

More Fiddling

Robina Russell, the daughter of a small country trader of Mid Yell brought a case of breach of promise against Thomas Williamson, another trader in a small way who lived across the Voe from the Russell family. In her summons, dated 9 November, 1871, she demanded that he pay her £100 damages and solatium (rather rasing the ante).[111] In his minute of defence Thomas's agent, Mr Sievwright, stated that though he called himself a merchant he was a poor man who had only recently set up a very small business which was not being very successful. Robina, he said, had not suffered any great injury, and he offered to compromise the case for £15. He was, he said, a poor man.[112] She knew that he was engaged to another girl to whom he was now married. In fact the case revealed a cat's cradle of emotional entanglements. Margery Mouat (the girl he later married) came from a comparatively well to do family on Unst with interests in a local chromate mine from which she hoped to inherit an interest. As he told Robina, he had broken off his engagement to marry her because he was afraid Margery might bring 'a case of damages' against him. Margery herself probably gained the idea from

109   SC 12/6/1870/4/27
110   SC 12/6/1870/4/34; SC 12/6/1870/36
111   SC 12/6/1871/60/1; SC 12/6/1871/60/3
112   SC 12/6/1871/60/13, pp.6-7.

Is this a lover's letter?

49

A legalistic letter from a wife who knew her rights.

her aunt Margaret Mouat of Unst who had brought a case of breach of promise in 1626.[113] And Robina took a leaf out of her book.

Witnesses were called. Robina's father, Robert, said that Thomas had been courting Robina until June, 1870, when they were to have married. He himself had gone to a great deal of expense in improving the house and buying food and drink for the wedding. A wedding dress was bought, and on the day it was shown to Thomas the engagement was broken off. He had been courting Miss Mouat before he got engaged to Robina, and was afraid she would pursue him if he persisted in his engagement to Robina, but he still 'came after her' with meaningless promises, and at last she realised they meant nothing. She suffered great distress, and her health suffered. Asked what she did with the wedding dress, he said 'she was sometimes thinking of burning it.' She had gone south to Edinburgh to work and to recover her health. Robina's mother confirmed his evidence: he would not marry Robina for fear Miss Mouat might bring an action of damages against him; her health and spirits had suffered seriously. This account of her daughter's sufferings was rudely interrupted by Thomas' agent, Sievwright, asking if Robina had not been courted by James Stewart in the past, and was he not courting her again? Her reply was a mournful reproach 'She will not be courting any more in this world.'[114]

The defence portrayed Robina as a philanderer. Thomas' brother Gavin said that she had corresponded not only with James Stewart, but with Gavin Harper, and had attempted to flirt with him too, saying she preferred him to his brother Thomas. She had been sweethearting James before she met Thomas, and returned to him when Thomas threw her over. She had not gone to Edinburgh for her health, but to meet James, who was a sailor, and when he returned from overseas, they travelled to Shetland together. Tamar Cooper said James had left his watch with her (as was the custom with seamen who were engaged); Jane M. Smith

113   SC 12/6/1826/32/1 see above, pp. 13-16, 'The Fiddler and the Virago'.
114   SC 12/6/1871/60/13, pp. 1-7.

confirmed that she had gone to Edinburgh to meet James; and Catherine Jamieson that they returned to Shetland together.[115]

Once married to Thomas Margery realised that her hoped-for patrimony would be vulnerable to his creditors, and needed to be protected. She wrote to Sievewright, her lawyer, and he pointed out to her father's trustees that her putative estate was protected under the Conjugal Rights (Scotland) Act, 1861.[116] Thomas could of course always persuade her to part with it, and perhaps he did.

On the 13th March 1872 the Sheriff Substitute, Andrew Mure made avizandum and pronounced his verdict. Thomas' tender was not legal. A tender ought to cover the pursuer's expenses, and must be paid as soon as agreed, but on his own admission the Defender was a poor man and could not pay it immediately. Therefore the Pursuer was granted £20 (not the £100 she had petitioned for). Thomas must pay her expenses, which came to £22-7-6. He reflected adversely on the morals of both, but especially on those of Thomas. The verdict 'must express disapprobation of the Defender's behaviour. His income was not high, and the small means of his wife, which were future and contingent, and which he might never touch, could not be considered. The sum now found due will hamper him in all probability for years to come.'[117]

This is not quite the end of the story., for Robina did not marry James Stewart, but in 1875 she married in Lerwick and emigrated to New Zealand. Her husband William Hughson, wrote poetry and was very religious, according to Wendy Gear, local historian of Yell.

Compromise Abandoned

In the third compromised case, unlike the first, the Defender admitted his guilt at once, and the case lasted only a few weeks. Like the earlier case it was triggered by a marriage, or rather, in this case, by an

115　SC 12/6/1871/60/15,16, and 17. For the deed of trust set up by Margery's father see MS Register of Deeds and Probative Wills in the Sheriff Court of Shetland, 5, fo. 286.
116　SC 12/6/1871/60/3 (unpaginated); SC 12/6/1871/60/28.
117　Information of Wendy Gear, local historian of Yell.

The eldest man involved in a case. William Duncan.

engagement.[118] Both parties lived in Burra Isle, a community of fishermen and crofters. In the 1871 Census William Duncan, aged 58, lived at Branchiclett and was described as a widower who shared his house with his daughter, a seaman's wife, and her family. They had two servants, and he was relatively well off. Agnes Goodlad, his intended bride, lived alone at Hamnavoe, Burra, and was a fish-curer aged 48. He started courting her in 1871, and on 12th May 1874 she brought a case against him in the Sheriff's Court for breach of promise, and asked for £50 damages.[119] She had no lengthy correspondence to prove his promises, such as Margaret Abernethy produced, but she had two documents which amounted to wills, though as they were unwitnessed, probably neither would have stood up in court. The second, dated 16 April, 1874, reads as follows:

> *This is to certfe that I William Duncan in my Sober Sence and Judgement Bequeathe the Sum of fifty Pounds Sterling to be paid to Augness Goodlad should I die beforew Marriage or if I die at any other time to be paid in full at my Death. But if she die before me nothing shall be paid to no pearson whoever that may interseed.*

> *This I declare in my own handwrite*

> *William Duncan*
> *Burra Isle*
> *Shetland*[120]

It had been folded carefully around a small studio portrait of William and placed in a small envelope. Once a treasure, it became a weapon.

What exactly happened between the will and Agnes' petition we cannot be sure, but on 11 May, 1874 William married Grace Humphrey, aged 44.[121] Agnes, of course, must have consulted her lawyer before that date to give the lawyer time to formulate the petition, but the day after

118   SC 12/6/1874/10/1. Here he is said to be a seaman and fisherman.
119   1 bid.
120   SC 12/6/1874/10/5.
121   Lerwick and Gulberwick Marriage Register

the wedding the summons to appear in court was issued and delivered to William. The sum she asked for was the same as William had promised her in his 'will' – £50.

The Minutes and Interlocutor provide us with the subsequent history of the case. On 27th May the case came up to court and a delay was granted as the parties were negotiating a compromise. On the 3rd of June William's defence was presented by his lawyer in standard lawyer's language. He admitted that the Defender had promised to marry the Pursuer, but had broken off the engagement because of 'public report' about the Pursuer's character. She had been 'carrying on illicit and improper intercourse with other men', and therefore when she brought the case 'to avoid the annoyance attending litigation' he offered to compromise the case for £20. This was refused, and he now tendered her £10, which he considered sufficient as neither her matrimonial prospects had suffered nor her feelings been wounded to that extent. He was also prepared to pay the expenses of the case and let her keep his watch, which was in her possession. The court now set the 7th of July for the parties to prove their statements. This would have involved both parties appearing personally and being subject to cross-examination as both parties could now be witnesses on a case of breach of promise. William immediately decided to retract his accusation of Agnes' improper intercourse and also to withdraw his offer to pay £20 plus expenses, and Agnes asked permission to abandon the case. The Sheriff discharged the order for proof, but William was ordered to pay Agnes £20 damages and *solatium*, and her expenses.[122] William's reluctance to appear in court may have been due to the fact that Shetland now had its own paper *The Shetland Times*, founded in 1872.

122   Bell, pp. 357-8; 37 & 38 Vict. c. 64; SC 12/6/1874/10/1

Chapter 5

The Newsworthy and the Un-newsworthy in the 1880s

The Widow's Daughter

The case of Joan Anderson, the daughter of Andrina Anderson, widow of the Widow's Asylum in Lerwick, against George Mackay, seaman of Lerwick was the first case in which both parties in a breach of promise case made use of the right to give evidence themselves under the 1874 Act. The bill had passed into law about the time Agnes Goodlad brought her case against William Duncan, and the prospect of facing Agnes in court was a reason he sought a compromise. In this case Joan and George not only gave evidence in court, but *The Shetland Times* gave an almost blow by blow account of the whole sorry business to a crowded court which regarded it as prime entertainment.[123]

Joan demanded £100 damages as a deeply wronged woman. In her condescendence she described how about March 1876 they had met. She was then a servant to the agent of the Union Bank in Lerwick. He went to sea soon after, and returned in March 1878, when he remained in Lerwick for about two nights. At this time he told her mother that the next time he returned home he would marry her. He went to sea again, and returned about a year later, in March 1879. He then went to Aberdeen where he drilled for a month (perhaps with the Merchant

---

123   *The Shetland Times*, 27 March 1880, p. 2

Marine?). When he returned he once again renewed his promise to marry, but after seeing her about three or four times he ceased visiting her.[124] During his absences, however, they had carried on a voluminous correspondence, which at this stage Joan made available to their lawyers.[125]

George's letters were the longest and most interesting of the sailors' letters, though like those of the other defenders they were semi-literate, often repetitive, with frequent requests for news of family and friends. Endearments abound, and rows of kisses conclude each letter. One of the first, written from Glasgow in July 1876 is fairly typical of the early letters.[126] It is written on embossed frilly pink paper intended to appeal to sailors, and carrying sentimental verse. This one was captioned 'To a Sailor's Lass' and opens with the following deathless lines:

Though far from thee I roam about the world,
Love keeps 'look out' and holds us both together,
And like the sails our hearts are closely furled ...

He remained 'truly to death', but the letter, though sentimental does not yet seem to focus on her specifically. He sent his 'kind love' to two other women as well. But should one not be surprised when he writes 'I was sorry that you and Ann More could not get a Smok of Tob from the Dutchmen but hold on and till I com hom and will bring you som'; it scarcely suggests Victorian values.

On the 13th October, 1877 he wrote from New Zealand on his frilly notepaper, clearly homesick:

Dear I don't think much of this country it is a wild looking place.
I saw som Shetland pople and they told me they wold like to com
back afin fro there is nothing to see hear but trees and hills and
every thing is so dear it is 2 the price there is nothing chape but
beef[127]

124 SC 12/6/1880/7/1
125 SC 12/6/1880/7/10-33
126 SC 12/6/1880/7/11
127 SC 12/6/1880/7/12

22a8

Port Chalmars Jan. 10 the

My Dear Joan

I write you again a few lins
I did not catch the last mail
I am well hopping this will
find you the same I supose
we will be home as soon as
you get this for this will not
leve hear till a week after
us so My Dear but I write
about the middle of March
I have now news to tell you
at this time I give you it
when I com hom so My Dear
Joan so Dear look out for
me about the first of Apial
if the stemmer coms in the
night I will clime over

Anticipating pleasure to come.

the wall and com and
Kias you whill your stepping
to look out that all now
Dear we are going to get up
the antler so thay are singing
ferwell to Duneden and
the Girls around cap
Horn   we are going away to day
         so yours truly Geo H c/ioq

x x x / x y x x x x x x x x x x x
        x x x x x x x x x x x x x

comming
Horn

Fond Hopes Destroyed

On the 12th November, 1877, in a Christmas letter he put a footnote which amounted to a somewhat off-hand proposal of marriage: 'I suppose all the young men will be getting married this winter surly our tim will com yet'[128]

His letters from New Zealand are unusual in sketching in the odd sentence the more newsworthy happenings on shipboard: the cook fell overboard and drowned when drunk; the crew had deserted; the captain had married. However the main thrust of the letters was courtship and marriage. However he had changed his mind about New Zealand and thought they should emigrate. On 7th November, 1878, he wrote from Port Chalmers:

I hop nixt time I com out hear I hop you will be com along with me for there is a grat many Shetland pople so I have seen a lot of them so thought say is the best I can do get marrid and com out hear one party said they would have a hous redy for us If I would send them word.[129]

On the 10th January, 1878, he wrote of coming home:

Dear look out for me about the first of April. If the stemmer coms in the night I will clime over the wall and com and kiss you whill your slepping so look owt that all now. Dear we are going to get up the anker so they are singing ferwell to Dunedin and the girls around Cap Horn.

The letter was decorated with many kisses, a drawing of a ship under full sail, and the words 'coming Hom.'[130]

He returned again in March '79 (the dating is Joan's), and went to Aberdeen, but after visiting her several times, he cooled off. Finally when asked for an explanation, he admitted he did not intend to marry her.[131]

---

128 SC 12/6/2880/7/13
129 SC 12/6/1880/7/23
130 SC 12/6/1880/7/22
131 Robertson, pp. 152-3; case collated from *The Shetland Times*, 27 March 1880, and evidence in SC 12/6/1880/7/34

The Widow's Daughter

Joan's case came up before Sheriff Rampini on Monday 22nd March, 1880. George attempted at first to deny how long he had known Joan. The first two letters were written in 1877, not in 1876. He had made a simple mistake. He had met Joan shortly before he left Lerwick. When he had returned in 1878 he saw her at her mother's house on the Sunday night. 'I did not promise to marry her. I said to her mother that I was going to take Joan from her. She answered that I would have to take her too. I laughed at her and went away.' He denied that he said he would marry her on his return. He saw her 'about Martinmas last'. Under cross-examination he said he was always drunk. He had been drunk the last time he saw her. She had haled him in the street and taken him home. He had been very drunk, and they had undressed him and put him to bed with Joan beside him. When he woke he got up and never went back. After that if she saw him in the street she would 'cry names as she passed'. According to Joan he had written to her from 1876, and she repeated much of the evidence in her condescendence, but elaborated on it, under cross-examination. In 1878 he had asked her mother for her hand, and Joan had accepted him. She had quarrelled with him about his drinking, and the last time he visited them he had been tipsy. He had come home with her and slept in the inner room. Under pressure she admitted she had slept there too, though without undressing. Further witnesses were produced by each party. Joan's mother Andrina confirmed her daughter's statement, whilst George insisted on his drunkenness.

Rampini found for the Pursuer, and awarded her £25 and £20.14s 1d in expenses. The breach of promise had gone practically uncontradicted, while the Defender had attempted, unsuccessfully, to prove he had been subjected to undue influence. He ended by condemning the lax morals of both parties.[132]

---

132   SC 12/6/1880/7/3

Thy form is ever near me

(1)
Thy form is ever near me
Though miles between us lie.
Thy sunny smile doth cheer me.
And check the rising sigh.
Again with thee, I wander
Where limpid waters stray.
Where we walked that winters ——
When you give yourself to me [evening]

Thy form is ever near me
Though miles between us lie
Thy sunny smile doth cheer me
And check the rising sigh

(2)
I hear the same sweet promise,
I heard on that last eve.,
When you vowed to be true
As I left you on the shore
And on that promise resting
Contented I'll remain
Till time very soon will will bring
Back to my love again [me]

(3)
Farewell we must be parted
Be parted for awhile
Be ever constant hearted

Poem – 'Thy form is ever near me'

I'll true to the remain
Forget notin my absence love
My heart still beats for thee
Rember dearest time will prove
How constant each will be

Minor Cases

After Joan Anderson's courtroom drama there were no more court cases for eight years, but in the interval there were six minor cases which never came to court. The first was that of Lillias Hay of Scatsta who brought two separate actions against Charles James Spence of Unst. The first was for aliment, the second for breach of promise, and both were heard on the same day, the 8th of January, 1883. The child had been born on the 14th of August 1881, and she petitioned for £2 inlying expenses for her illegitimate son, £1 a year in quarterly instalments to the age of seven, or until he could support himself.[134] For damages she asked for £100. In both cases she asked for expenses, and the freezing of his assets. Charles put in notices of appearance to defend himself, but no further documents have been found. Perhaps she did not pursue the case any further, but it is as likely that the rest of the processes were lost. Sheriff Court records for some years are rather scanty. We cannot fill out Lillias Hay's case from any letters, though in her condescendence for damages she mentions a voluminous correspondence.[133]

In the next case, which resembles it in some ways, save that a number of letters survived. Bruce Barclay of Whalsay brought a case for breach of promise against William Breck, a cooper of Freefields Dock, Lerwick the following year, on the 28th of October, 1884. And a separate case for aliment followed about six months later.[134] They had met in August, 1883 when he was working at Whalsay as a cooper there. He went to Lerwick in October, and she went to visit him for a week from the 1st of November, and he seduced her. On a later visit she had stayed with a Catharine Brothwick. He visited her again in Whalsay, and she told him she was pregnant, and he promised to marry her at Christmas. 'He has since then married another woman.'[135]

---

133   SC 12/6/1883/2/1; SC 12/6/1883/4/1
134   SC 12/6/1884/55/1; SC12/6/1885/27
135   SC 12/6/1884/55/1

Minor Cases

In many breach of promise cases the letters covered a very long period: William's cover a much shorter period. What is striking about the letters is that they are better spelt than those of the sailors, though some lapses may be due to drink, a subject on which she upbraided him.[136] But even more interesting and ominous is the fact that he never mentions her pregnancy. The last letters show a falling off in affection. This was presaged in some verses he sent her in his letter of the 17th of December 1883, one of his last:

Farewell we must be parted
Be parted for a while
Be ever constant hearted
I'll true to thee remain
Forget not in my absence love
My heart still beats for thee
Remember dearest love will tell
How constant each will be.[137]

William entered a notice of appearance for the breach of promise case, but it does not seem to have been pursued, or once again the later processes were lost. However, Bruce may have been more successful with the aliment case. William failed to put in an appearance so declaring his guilt, so she petitioned to be 'granted her crave', that is the amounts mentioned in her petition: £2 inlying expenses, plus £4 a year for ten years, and her expenses, which came to £3. 1s. This would depend on whether, as she had asked, his assets had really been frozen, and were adequate to pay up over the years.

There were further minor cases which are incomplete or were not pursued, two in 1887 and two in 1891. There is little to be learned from these, and they have not been discussed.

---

136   Probably because education had improved as a result of improving standards of education in Scotland. H. Corr, 'An exploration into Scottish Education', *People and Society in Scotland, 1830-1914*, vol 2, ed. W.H Fraser and R. J. Morris (John Donald, publishers. Ltd, 1990), pp. 294-5
137   I doubt if this was his own composition, though the punctuation is all his own. SC 12/6/1884/55/10

Chapter 6

The Limits of the Courts Clarified

In the next three breach of promise cases women had not been very successful and in these next cases we see the limits of the courts in righting wrongs demarcated and limited. The first shows again the full power of the court. The second its power and determination to enforce its will by imposing a gaol sentence, and the third by showing the limits within which the law could operate.

'Bina the rumbustuous virgin[138]

This case involved two cousins. In 1888 Robina Morrison, daughter of Robert Morrison of Tubie in Weisdale, brought a case against Arthur Tait, who lived with his father at Houll in the same parish. In her petition she asked for £50 damages.[139] However, apart from the years he was away at sea there was not much they agreed on.

Arthur had written many letters to Bina when he had been away, but it was quite difficult for his own advocate to get him to admit the fact.[140] If they were his he had forgotten. He did not keep copies. If they were his they were not serious. His absurd evasions convulsed the court, as this interchange shows:

---

138   The historian John Graham tells me she was known in the family as Bina. As there were four
       Robinas who brought important cases I shall refer to her as Bina throughout. We have already
       examined the case of Robina Russell. and the cases of Robina Hughson. and Robina Georgeson
       are still to come.
139   SC 12/6/1888/12/1
140   *Shetland News*, 16 June 1888 p.8; cf. SC 12/6/1888/10, pp. 1-22

'Bina the Rumbustuous Virgin'

'They were written just as a boyish adventure.' (Laughter.)
Mr MacGregor (for the defence) – 'Sailors must have sweethearts'. (Laughter.)
Witness – 'Certainly'. (Laughter).
The Sheriff – 'They should stick to them then'.

He had first gone abroad about nineteen years ago, and returned the following spring. From then on they were to correspond 'as betrothed lovers.' He returned from his second trip in 1874 and according to Bina he promised to marry her many times, but he put off doing so, until at last in 1875 he said he would do so the following winter. All this Arthur denied. Before he left he gave her a locket and chain, but according to Arthur it was she who had asked him for it. He had gone away to Australia for ten years. During his absence, according to Arthur, he had given up writing to her after five years because he had heard of the way she was behaving and her drinking. Robina did not mention any gap in their correspondence. On his return to Shetland in 1885 she said he visited her again, and promised to marry her after the harvest. She made ready once again, but though he visited her constantly, he put the wedding off from month to month. She had seen him at a ball at Christmas in 1887 when he had been rude to her. He was drunk. They had left together, and they had walked part of the way home together with others, and they had both fallen into a ditch. (When she mentioned this in court she joined in the laughter.) But they made it up afterwards. They were still to marry. Arthur denied all the promises to marry, but not having seen her that Christmas. She had been drunk and violent on that occasion, and they had not made it up afterwards. He had since married another woman.[141]

Mr MacGregor, Arthur Tait's lawyer summed up her character: 'She was shown to be a woman of violent temper, and addicted to swearing, and she had developed a liking for strong drink'. Mr

141   SC 12/6/1888/12/10, pp. 1-38.

67

Anderson, acting for Bina said that was no grounds for a breach of promise case. She was just 'a jolly hilarious woman.'[142] Mr. Mackenzie, the Sheriff-Substitute awarded Bina £10 in damages, plus expenses, but Arthur appealed, and on the ninth of August, 1888 Sherff Thoms gave his verdict. He increased the damages to £15. 'A more cruel charge than this unfounded one by the Defender against the woman who had at one time been the object of his affections, the Sheriff in his long experience never met with.'[143]

According to John Graham memories of the case lingered in the Defender's family, which felt deeply shamed by the case. Bina had turned up at the wedding dressed more grandly than the bride. She was a large woman and a flamboyant character. She described Arthur's bride as 'nae but a quarter o' tae.'

Poor Janet and the defaulting sailor

As Arthur Tait's assets had been frozen there would have been no serious problem in Bina being paid her damages and expenses, for he and his family were fairly reasonably well off. James Johnson seems to have suffered for his heartlessness and foolishness.

Janet Williamson, spinster of Neepaback near Burravoe, Yell, brought a case against James Johnson, sailor, of Firthness, North Delting on the second of February 1890. He had broken his promise to marry her though she had borne his child in December, 1885, and he refused to support it. Because Janet was very poor, to bring a case against James she went to her parish minister, Mr Watson and got a certificate from him vouching for her poverty, and she was put on the Poor's Roll. The couple were summoned to be examined by the Agents for the Poor, but James did not appear.[144]

142 *Shetland News*, 23.6.1888, p. 5
143 SC 12/6/1888/12/3; *Shetland News*, 13.8.1888, 7.7.1888, p. 5. For Thoms see Robertson, p. 211.
144 SC 12/6/1890/20/1; SC 12/6/1890/20/2

Poor Janet and the defaulting sailor

Janet was now in a position to bring a breach of promise case against James. In her petition she asked for £2 inlying expenses, and £6. 10s. for the child for 10 years. As the child had been born in 1885 she was due for £32.10s back pay. She asked for £200 in damages, and expenses, with interest on all these sums. She was out for vengeance, it is clear, and would screw him for every penny she could get, though she would be aware she would not get £200 – that was a frightener. She had certainly been deeply wronged, for it had been a long engagement. They had first met ten years ago, and became engaged two years later, in 1882. He had gone to sea in 1883, and they had corresponded. In early 1885 he stayed with her and they 'had Connection', words clearly put in her mouth by her lawyer, Mr Small. She had only allowed it because she relied on his marrying her. When she realised she was pregnant she told him, but he made excuses. He said he had no place to take her. He went to sea again in 1886 and seems to have cooled off. When he came back he brought his newly married wife. A summons was issued to James.[145]

James ignored it, and in December, 1890 Mr Small petitioned the court again. If he failed to respond to the court again or prove that his failure to pay had not been wilful, he should be sent to prison. Sheriff-substitute Mackenzie examined both parties, and decided that James' refusal to pay was wilful, and sentenced him to six weeks in prison, or until he paid up, or Janet forgave him his debts.[146] It seems unlikely that Janet would be prepared to let him off lightly.

The Saddest Case; Walter v James

Robina III died of puerperal fever two days after her illegitimate child, who was stillborn. Her father, Walter Hughson, of Ogilvy's Buildings,

145   SC 12/6/1890/28/1
146   SC 12/6/1890/62/1. A very similar case was brought the following year, and reported in *The Shetland Times*, 14 February 1891. The Debtors' Act (Scotland), 43&44 Vict. c. 34 covered cases of refusal to pay aliment (*Bell*, p.463).

Fond Hopes Destroyed

Lerwick, brought a case against James Smith, a seaman of Queen's Lane, Lerwick. This brief case for breach of promise was reported in the local papers.

According to Walter's condescendence Robina and James had met in the winter of 1888-9, and he had courted her assiduously. He promised to marry her before he left for St. John's in January 1890, and again on his return. He said he had arranged to rent a house – which Walter did not quite believe. She was in service until February, 1890, and after that lived with her father until her death. Trusting to James' promise to marry her she had allowed him to seduce her first in August 1889 and thereafter, including that Christmas. On the 30th of August, 1890, she had a still-born child, and died two days later. Walter asked for £50 damages and *solatium*. He had suffered in his feelings through her seduction and death, and through the loss of her services and company. He also asked to be recompensed for the expenses of her lying-in and the burial of mother and child.[147] He handed in an itemised account, amounting to £4 8s:[148]

Dr Skae's account for medical attendance	*£1.10*
Nurse	*15*
J. Hutchinson for daughters coffin	*1.6.6*
Coffin for child	*4*
Interment fees of daughter in Lerwick New Cemetery	*5*
Do child	*2.6*
Sundry outlays	*5*

James' denial was total. He was not the father. The father was Andrew Mann. He had not spent Christmas with Robina. He had spent it in his own house 'having been assisted there by his friends in 'a state of intoxication.'[149]

---

147   SC 12/6/1891/15/1
148   SC 12/6/1891/15/3
149   SC 12/6/1891/15/7

70

On the fourth of April Sheriff Substitute Mackenzie heard the preliminary pleas. There would be no grounds for the case if James were not the father, but he saw no reason why Robina's father should not claim the expenses of the mother's inlying and of the funerals of mother and child. However, the Pursuer, Walter Hughson had claimed damages. The question whether one person could claim for another was difficult. These questions might be better settled after the facts were ascertained and the evidence heard. James Smith appealed to Sheriff Thoms himself, and the appeal was dismissed on the fourth of May. The case was to have come up before the Court on the 13th of May, but by then he had gone overseas, and he remained away. Walter finally abandoned the case in October 1893.[150]

The Biter Bit – a Cautionary Tale

The case of Robina Georgeson of Neep, Sandness against Arthur Walterson, a sailor of Houll, Sandness aroused considerable interest, not only because it was a breach of promise case which ran its full course in *The Shetland Times* and *Shetland News*, but also because it aroused controversy which resulted in a contempt of court case against *The Shetland Times*, and involved well known persons. It is notable too as being only the second case of breach of promise brought in nineteenth century Shetland which was won by the defender.

Robina was about four years older than Arthur, and they had been at school together, at the S.P.C.K. school at Sandness kept by Robert Jamieson, where she was a contemporary of his daughter Christina Jamieson, later secretary of the Shetland Women's Suffrage Society.[151] It becomes clear in the evidence that she never benefited from her education, and she was pitifully self-deluding.

---

150   SC 12/6/1891/15/5; *Shetland News*, 11.4.91. p. 8; SC 12/6/1891/15/10
151   L. Leneman, *A Guid Cause. The Women's Suffrage Movement in Scotland* (Aberdeen University Press, 1991), p. 262.

The opening shots in the case was a series of letters from Mr. Grierson, Robina's solicitor, to Arthur Walterson. On the 21st March 1894 Mr Grierson wrote to Arthur to warn him that she would bring a case of breach of promise against him unless he would pay her £100 damages and *solatium*, or implement his engagement. 'It is not Miss Georgeson's wish to expose you, but in view of the very cruel and unmanly way you have treated her.' Arthur's reply to this letter, which had verged on blackmail, was a denial that there had been a promise[152]. Grierson tried to tighten the screw. On the 14th of April he wrote to Arthur that Miss Georgeson told him that there was a rumour that she had been to Dr. Elder at Walls to get something to induce an abortion, implying that she was a loose woman, and guilty of a criminal act. If Arthur did not reveal the source of this rumour he would be sued for £100 for defamation.[153]

However, Robina was impatient. She brought a case for breach of promise on the 18th of April, 1894.[154] In her petition she again demanded £100 damages. According to her condescendence she was living with her mother at Neep. In the winter of 1890-91 the defender had started courting her. She was then working at Melby House whose laird had married her sister. The defender was a sailor and earned good wages at sea and she had returned to live with her mother after leaving Melby. At Melby they slept together in the same room as two other servant girls who shared another bed. At home, as at Melby he proposed to her, and she accepted him. The marriage was no secret. He left to go to sea in the spring of 1891 and asked her to correspond with him. When he returned about the tenth of January 1894 he told her 'he could not marry at present, but he would next winter.' Shortly after this he started courting someone else.

152   SC 12/6/1894/24/11; SC 12/6/1894/24/14
153   SC 12/6/1894/24/12; (on Elder) *Manson's Almanack and Directory for 1896* (Lerwick, T. and J. Manson, 1896), p. 55
154   SC 12/6/1894/24/1

The Biter Bit – a Cautionary Tale

The case itself opened on the 19th of May, 1894, and evidence for the Pursuer was led by Mr Grierson. Robina confirmed her condescendence and was cross-examined by Mr. Robertson on various matters. She could not read or write and Elizabeth Jamieson had acted as her amanuensis, writing the letters at her dictation and reading Arthur's replies to her. She denied that she told the Defender she had slept with one of her cousins, and had wished to sue him because he abandoned her because she was sleeping with another man, but she did not deny that she had shown the Defender letters he had written to her. Did she remember a letter from the Defender 'saying he had never intended to marry her and would not?' Grierson had barely started to re-examine her when she collapsed, and could not go on. She was recalled later, but added nothing substantial.[155]

Mr Scott, the laird of Melby gave evidence very much in her defence. He confirmed her evidence on Arthur's visits to Melbie. 'It was a usual thing for young people courting to sleep together. I would not have allowed the Defender to come as he did if I had not thought he intended to marry her,' and Robina had told him they were to marry. He took a brotherly interest in her, more or less as a guardian. 'Considering the climate of Shetland and the lack of facilities for intercourse, the so-called Shetland Courtship may mean nothing more than lad and lass making acquaintanceship. It does not of necessity mean courtship with a view to marry.' Robina's mother remembered him staying overnight on his return home and leaving in the morning 'nowise bashful'. But she never heard him promise to marry her daughter; whilst Elizabeth Jamieson her amanuensis could not remember 'anything between them in the letters'.[156]

Arthur Walterson gave his evidence in a straightforward way, later commented on by the Sheriff. He confirmed the dates of events and

---

155   SC 12/6/1894/24/17, pp. 1-10; *Shetland News*, 26 May 1894, pp. 7-8
156   SC 12/6/1894/24/17, pp. 10-12, 23-4, 27; Robertson, pp. 171-2

sleeping arrangements and not much else. The purpose of his visits was larking with the Pursuer. She had asked him to correspond with her when he went to sea. When he addressed her as 'sweetheart' in his letters, what did it mean? He had meant simply 'friend'. His reason for corresponding with her had been 'to hear larks, and news, and so on like that.' She wrote asking him if he was thinking of marrying, but he told her it was for him to decide. He admitted though, he had never promised to marry her, 'but at one time I had an affection for the girl, but it gradually decreased during the correspondence…'[157]

Proof was interrupted to await the hearing of two sailors who were to return to give evidence The court in the end lost patience, but before it resumed on the 3rd of July a letter to *The Shetland Times* gave a new complication to the case, and this resulted in a case of contempt of court. On the 9th of June a letter appeared in the paper from Mrs Jessie Saxby, an Unst-born author who sprang to the defence of Shetland womanhood against the aspersions cast on them by Mr Scott in his evidence on 'Shetland Courtships'. One result of this was to provide many column inches in the correspondence columns debating that subject over the next weeks (readers of that paper still being anxious to debate contentious matters, such as udal law, in its columns.) More seriously it resulted in a case of contempt of court being brought on the 16th of June against Mrs Saxby and the proprietors of *The Shetland Times*.[158] The Sheriff however regarded it as an 'indiscretion', and 'he hoped that evidence would flow as spontaneously as it had done'.[159]

The Defence witnesses were three aged people who had grown up in Sandness. It was their opinion that courtship could mean much or nothing; it might be simply a lark, and did not imply a promise to marry.[160] Hay Shennan, the Sheriff was of much the same opinion. He

---

157   SC 12/6/ 1894/24/17, pp. 12-21
158   It was not the first time it had been discussed. Its prevalence had been commented on during an aliment case in 1889 by the lawyer Mr Macwatt (*The Shetland Times*, 9.3.1889) Not long after the poor man drowned in a boating accident attempting to rescue a friend. (Robertson, p. 119).
159   *Shetland News*, 16.6.1894; SC 12/6/1894/24/18
160   SC 12/6/1894/24/17, pp. 23-33

decided the Pursuer had not proved her case, and awarded Arthur Walterson his expenses which amounted to £31.9.9. There had been no promise to marry her 'As far as promise to marry is concerned, such winter courtships may mean nothing more than a summer flirtation elsewhere.'[161]

---

161   SC 12/6/1894/24/3; *Shetland News*, 27.10.1894; SC 12/6/1894/24/25; Robertson, p. 173.

Chapter 7

More Compromise

After 1874 there had been no more attempts to settle cases out of court for a quarter of a century. Why this should be so is unclear, but the last case of the nineteenth century and the first of the twentieth century involved compromises. The dramatic cases of 1880, 1888 and 1894, which the public had enjoyed as popular entertainments probably influenced them. Settling out of court was more seemly.

A Clinical Case

The first of these occurred in 1899. Annie Johnston and John Johnson both came from Bouster on Yell. She was the eldest daughter of a widow in comfortable circumstances, and he a petty officer on a steamship trading to America. In her Condescendence, dated 14th February, 1899, she gives her version of events. They were in their late twenties and had grown up together. Before he had gone to sea six years ago he had started corresponding with her, and about two years ago he had sent her an engagement ring. When he came back, trusting his promise to marry she had submitted to his embraces. Before he went to sea again he gave her a watch, and after he left she found she was pregnant, and she wrote and told him. He wrote back in June 1898 to say he would marry her when he returned, and he wrote similarly to his parents. She gave birth to a daughter that August. When he returned in November 1898 he refused or delayed to fulfill his promise, and since then he had failed to pay her inlying expenses or provide for alimenting the child. She had also incurred expenses in buying clothes for the wedding. The Defender ought to pay £2 inlying expenses, £6 a year for ten years from the birth of the child, as aliment, in quarterly instalments, £100 damages, and the expenses of the case.[162]

The Summons was dispatched immediately, and on the 28th of January John entered his Notice of Appearance.[163] He put in no defence, but immediately suggested a compromise. Annie was prepared to cooperate, and on the 1st of February they entered into negotiations. A month later they tendered a Joint Minute to the Court: John was to pay £2 in inlying expenses, aliment at £4 a year for the first five years, and thereafter £5 by equal quarterly instalments to the age of ten. Damages were set at £30, and Annie was allowed the expenses of the case. The case appears to have been singularly free from animus, and was dealt with with almost clinical efficiency.[164]

A Broken Triangle

The last of these cases occurred in 1900. Miss Mary Jane Smith initiated the case against William Harper with a petition dated 30th April, 1900. She worked as a domestic servant for John Bruce Esq. of Sumburgh, and William was a fisherman and seaman from nearby Scatness. They were 29 and 30 respectively. In 1897 he proposed to her, and they began to correspond 'on the footing of engaged persons'. William knew when he proposed to her that James Young had been courting her, and asked her to make a choice between them, and on faith of his promise of marriage she had done so. However, the marriage planned for that November had to be postponed. Mrs Bruce promised her if she delayed her marriage until Mrs Bruce returned from a trip down South she would 'make the wedding.' Then William wanted to delay the wedding whilst he went to the fishing. She saw him

162   SC 12/6/1899/2/1
163   SC 12/6/1899/2/2
164   SC 12/6/1899/2/3; SC 12/6/1899/2/4

77

occasionally in Lerwick during August where their friends and relatives regarded them as engaged. During this time he was very affectionate and spoke of the considerable sums of money he was saving, and consequently she bought a wedding dress and various household goods. But when the fishing season ended, and without telling her, he went to Plymouth to a training ship as a member of the Royal Navy Reserve, giving her the impression he had done so under orders. But this was not true. He now refused to marry her, and she demanded £200 in damages.[165] William told a very different story.[166] According to him Mary Jane had asked him to visit her, and he did so occasionally until James Young's arrival. He had been paying his attentions to Mary Jane formerly, and William objected. She led him to believe that all communication had ended, and William agreed to continue seeing her. In the winter of 1897 he went to Lerwick to train with the Royal Naval Reserve, and whilst there heard she had been seeing James. He asked her to give him back his letters, and she gave him two, saying (as we shall see, falsely) these were all she had, and he destroyed them. He had never asked her to marry him. Since then he had received a letter from her dated the 6th of February, 1900 which made no mention of his alleged promise, or of marriage. 'The Pursuer bids him goodbye, talks of going away, and hopes she may meet him, if not here, in some other place'.

Before the record was closed on the 6th of June 1900 Mary Jane reaffirmed her case and denied that 'either by letter or any other method' she had released William from his promise.[167] Before their averments could be put to the proof in the usual way for a case of damages though, *The Shetland Times* had set up in type a report of the case, but before it was published they were forced to remove the names of the parties concerned, because they had been informed that the case

---

165 SC 12/6/1900/6/1
166 SC 12 June 1900/6/4
167 SC 12/6/1900/6/1, p.10 (in margin)

was to be settled out of court.[168] Who leaked the story is not known. The information was correct. William Harper had tendered a minute on the 14th of June, and about a fortnight later the court accepted a more satisfactory joint minute, and Mary Jane was awarded £40 damages.[169]

168 *Shetland Times*, 23/6/1900, p.5
169 SC 12/6/1900/6/6; SC 12/6/1900/6/14

Chapter 8

Counting the Cost

After a case ended the pursuer must have considered what she had gained and what she had lost. Had her reputation been restored, had she seen her fickle lover suffer sufficiently, were damages sufficient balm for her wounded feelings? Those questions were all interrelated. The restitution of her reputation was expressed by the size of the damages the judge awarded her, supposing that she won her case. The punishment of the defender was also reflected by the size of this award. There were, however, other factors to play in such case.

Damages will be considered first. Actually what a woman was awarded bore very little relation to what she demanded in her petition. The most modest demands were made by two paupers. Barbara Smith had petitioned for £30, but she was awarded only £1. This was half the amount she was granted yearly as aliment.[170] In 1887 Christina Duncan petitioned for a mere £25, but as the defender did not appear we do not know what the judge would have given her.[171] The highest sum any pursuer petitioned for was £200. This was settled by compromise for £40, and not by a decision of the court.[172] Some petitions were for £100, and most for £50. Ann Jamieson, who petitioned for £50 and was granted £25, won more than most.[173] The average for Shetland was £20. This was much lower than in England where the average was £200.[174] Ginger Frost describes the women as normally working class or lower

170   SC 12/6/1828/85/3
171   SC 12/6/1887/81/1
172   SC 12/6/1900/6/1; SC 12/6/1900/6/14
173   SC 12/6/1867/4/3
174   Frost, pp. 224-5

middle class. One wonders if the defendants ever paid. There were, though, cccasional cases where far higher damages were granted, as in the cause célèbre, Foote v. Hayne, where the fashionable actress Maria Foote was awarded £3,000.[175]

Whether these awards were realistic or not, the value of the awards of damages in Shetland seems to have borne some relation to the sort of wages women could earn there. But records on work still need to be found. They appear to be scanty and scattered. The only full records which have turned up so far are the records of Veensgarth farm workers in the mid nineteenth century, and the records of fish gutters. The Veensgarth farm workers accounts list women's pay at 8d a day, or 10d a day during the harvest. Work was seasonal, and the wage for two days work in January would be 1s 4d. A girl who worked the full six days at the harvest would get 5s a week. But the work was casual and most worked only a few days even at this time.[176] The work of fish curers was also casual and seasonal. Jim Coull who has studied the records of one large fish curer has estimated that in 1883 in a three-month season a girl might earn 10s to 15s a week.[177] Obviously damages were a small fortune to pursuers who received them. If the men were able to pay is less certain.

Restoring her reputation was a major concern in bringing a case, for it did no good to a woman to be 'brought into the mouth of the public' to use again Ann Jamieson's vivid phrase. Ann herself was able to establish that she had been hard done by. She was awarded £25 'a fair and legitimate and not merely a nominal amount'.[178] With her reputation restored she seems to have been able to get a job with Adies, the general merchant at Voe.[179] In another case the same year another woman was awarded the same sum which was seen by the Sheriff to be 'very

175   S. L. Steinbach, 'The melodramatic contract; Breach of Promise and the performance of virtue' (*Nineteenth Century Studies*, Hammond, Louisiana University), vol. 14, 2000, p. 4
176   Shetland Archives, D. 31/18/15
177   J. Coull, 'Herring gutters in Unst during the herring boom' *Shetland Life*, Sept. 2002, pp. 16-18
178   SC 12/6/1867/4/20, pp. 13-15; SC 12/6/1867/4/3 (unpaginated)
179   Repored by G.P.F Peterson – local historian

moderate'.[180] The most complete exoneration came however in a case in 1888 where the pursuer, Robina Morrison was slandered by the defender Arthur Tait in his evidence. Nevertheless the Sheriff-Substitute only awarded her £10. The Sheriff-Substitute who tried the case was a new one, and he took into account the fact that whilst Arthur Tait had been at sea for many years he had returned some time ago, so that she should have had time to realise he had cooled off; hence, taking her position in life into consideration, the Sheriff-Substitute awarded her £10, but the Sheriff increased it to £15.[181] In bringing a case however, a woman might well fail to rescue her reputation, for her own behaviour might be criticised. Robina Russell petitioned for £100 in 1871, but the Sheriff was not impressed. He said 'the case disclosed no serious cause of damages'. She had been two-timing the defender (who had also two-timed her). Damages 'need not be weighed in fine scales'. Nevertheless she got £20.[182] Possibly the Sheriff was swayed by a pretty face. The 1880 case of Joan Anderson, who also petitioned for £100, is equally puzzling. The Sheriff describes her morals as no better than those of the Defender, and 'of the laxest', yet she was awarded the same as the virtuous women of 1867.[183] Perhaps the court was not to be regarded as a court to decide on matters of morals in general. The length of the engagement weighed heavily in these three cases.

Revenge was sweet, and as well as seeing the satisfaction of winning damages and securing her reputation the women sought to punish and humiliate the men who had jilted them. Even before a case was brought a woman could spread damaging rumours. According to William Nisbet, Margaret Mouat had managed to prevent him finding employment.[184] The court offered further humiliation as the audience regarded cases of breach of promise as entertainment, and particularly enjoyed a defender's love letters. Arthur Tait's letters to his 'dear love'

180   SC 12/6/1867/2/3
181   SC 12/6/1888/12/3
182   SC 12/6/1871/60/3
183   SC 12/6/1888/7/3; *Shetland Times*, 27 March 1880; p.2
184   SC 12/6/1826/32/4

were punctuated with gales of laughter when read aloud in court.[185] Yet such humiliation as the man suffered in court was nothing to what the girl suffered in being jilted. Many other women must have been abandoned by fickle lovers without bringing cases, and a handful started cases and lost heart, or gave way to social pressure. It took real courage to bring a case.

In the nineteenth century after the secularisation of the action for breach of promise it became easier for women to bring actions, and it provided a potent tool. Twenty-five Shetland women brought cases, but we do not know if this was a high proportion compared with elsewhere in Scotland. In the twentieth century there were three cases by 1922 in Shetland. They probably decrease thereafter, but the evidence is not yet available. The action was abolished in Scotland in 1984. It was then considered (condescendingly) that it 'may once have been useful but it is now inconsistent with the modern position of Women.'[186] Whether this is true is perhaps debatable.

---

185   SC 12/6/1888/12/10, pp. 1-22; *Shetland News*, 16 June 1888, p. 8
186   Law Reform (Husband and Wife) (Scotland) Act 1984 (c. 15)

Bibliography

Shetland Island Archives
  The Census, 1841-1900 (on microfilm)
  CH2/1072/3, 13, (Lerwick Kirk Sessions Records)
  D. 1/228/6 J. Mitchell and Sons Herring Book
  D.8/400/16 Bruce of Sumburgh. Duties of a chambermaid
  D. 31/18/15 Women's Labour, Veeensgarth
  SC 12/6/1798-1900, Sheriff Court Processes
  Old Parochial Registers to 1854 (Microfilms from the General
  Register Office)
Shetland News
The Shetland Times
Lerwick Marriage Registry
  Many of these are held by the Lerwick Registrar of Births,
  Deaths and Marriages. A list of local registrars is available.

Books and Articles

Bell's Dictionary and Digest of the Laws of Scotland, ed.G.Watson
  (Bell and Barfute, Edinburgh, 1852)
M. Bochel, *'Dear Gremista'. The Story of the Nairn Fisher Girls at
  the Gutting* (National Museum of Antiquities of Scotland, for the
  Nairn Fishertown Museum, 1979)
J. R. Coull, 'Herring gutters in Unst during the herring boom'
  (*Shetland Life*, September, 2002 pp. 16-18)
M. Flinn, ed., *Scottish Population History*, (Cambridge, 1977)
P. Fraser, 'Old-Time Shetland Day Wedding' (*Shetland Folk Book*, 3,
  1957)
G. S. Frost, *Promises Broken: Courtship, Class and Gender in
  Victorian England* (Charlottesville, VA, 1995)
G. S. Frost, 'I shall not sit down and crie'. Women, Class and Breach
  of Promise of Marriage Plaintiffs in England (*Gender and History*
  6, 1994)

Glossary of Scottish Legal Terms (Law Society of Scotland, Butterworths, Edinburgh, 1992)

J. W. Irvine *Lerwick and the Birth and Growth of an Island Town* (Lerwick Community Council, 1995)

C. Jamieson, 'The Women of Shetland' (*The New Shetlander*, no. 177, 1991)

A. Johnson, 'Whatever became of Janet Duncan' (*Shetland Folk Book* 9, 1995)

Law Reform (Husband and Wife) (Scotland) Act 1984 (c.15)

L. Leneman, *A Guid Cause. The Women's Suffrage Movement in Scotland* (Aberdeen University Press, 1991)

R. Mitchison and L. Leneman, *Sexuality and Control.* Scotland 1660-1780 (Basil Blackwell, 1989)

Report of the Scottish Law Commission on the outdated Rules in the Law of Husband and Wife, (no. 76, 1983)

M. S. Robertson, *Sons and Daughters of Shetland* (Shetland Publishing Company, 1991)

Second Report of the Commissioners appointed to inquire into the Truck System (Shetland) (Edinburgh 1872) Reprinted by Thuleprint Ltd, Sandwick, Shetland, 1978.

H. Shennan, *A Judicial Maid of all Work* (William Hodge and Co. Ltd, Edinburgh and Glasgow, 1933)

B. Smith 'Kirstie Caddell's Christmas' (*Shetland Folk Book* 8, 1988)

T. C. Smout 'Aspects of Sexual Behaviour in Scotland' in A. A. Maclaren, ed., *Social Class in Scotland* (John Donald, Edinburgh, 1974)

S. L. Steinbach, 'The Melodramatic Contract. Breach of Promise and the Performance of Virtue' *Nineteenth Century Studies*, 1 (South Eastern University, Louisiana, U.S.A.

S. Telford, *In a World a wir ane. A Shetland Herring Girl's Story* (The Shetland Times Ltd., 1998)

W. Dove Wilson, *The Practice of the Sheriff Courts in Scotland in Civil Causes* (3rd edn., Bell and Barfute, Edinburgh, 1883)